Foundation design
simply explained

JOHN FABER

B.Sc., F.I.C.E., F.I.Struct.E., M.Cons.E.,

and

BRIAN JOHNSON

M./ M.A., M.I.C.E., M.Inst.H.E.

SECOND EDITION

OXFORD UNIVERSITY PRESS

1976

Oxford University Press, Ely House, London W. 1

GLASGOW NEW YORK TORONTO MELBOURNE WELLINGTON
CAPE TOWN IBADAN NAIROBI DAR ES SALAAM LUSAKA ADDIS ABABA
DELHI BOMBAY CALCUTTA MADRAS KARACHI LAHORE DACCA
KUALA LUMPUR SINGAPORE HONG KONG TOKYO

ISBN 0 19 859513 1

© Oxford University Press 1976

Typeset by EWC Wilkins Ltd., London and Northampton
Printed in Great Britain by Fletcher & Son Ltd., Norwich

Preface

The first edition of this small book was conceived in 1959, when soil mechanics was becoming a popular subject the ordinary engineer and architect could no longer afford to ignore. The purpose of the book was to set down *simply* the problems that normally arise in designing foundations, and the various ways in which these problems can be tackled. It was never the aim that the book should refer to the more obscure problems, and no pretence was made that the subject had been treated exhaustively. Nevertheless, care was taken to avoid half-truths creeping in.

Now after 15 years the earlier magic of soil mechanics can be seen in its truer perspective as a means of providing supporting information to back up the engineers' broader judgement and experience. The practical value of loading tests has retained its proper place, and so has recognition of the need for the engineer to go and see for himself, on site, the actual conditions and ground exploration works, making use of his own feel for the situation with his own observations and commonsense. We also have now a later British Standard (CP 2004 (1972) *Foundations*).

In these circumstances, a second edition of the book has been suggested. The aim has been to bring things sensibly up-to-date, but only in so far as developments and practice have become reliably established. More detailed information is given for the theories of foundations on clays; and modified coefficients are shown for soils which are both cohesive and frictional. For sands, mention is made of the Dutch cone test which is starting to make inroads here into the popularity of the standard penetration test. The matter of consolidation settlement is gone into in greater detail, both in terms of its significance and methods of forecasting. Pore-water pressure is discussed in relation to the consolidation of clays. More emphasis is placed on the influence of ground-water. Cast-*in-situ* piles have greatly increased in popularity over precast piles.

The preparation of this new edition coincides with the move in Britain from Imperial units to SI units. The SI units are basically metric and enjoy the decimal system; yet they differ from the European c.g.s. system in that they introduce a fresh concept for the unit of force, known as the newton. This is roughly equal to the pull on a $\frac{1}{4}$ lb mass, and for convenience of memory coincides approximately with the weight of an apple!

Also at the present time we are moving our thoughts on reinforced concrete design into the new ways of British Standard CP 110 (1972): *The structural use of concrete,* where philosophy relates to the limit state, with the application of partial safety factors. This could produce some confusion in foundation design, where — instead of applying such a partial safety factor to the characteristic load — a load factor is applied to the soil's *ultimate* bearing capacity to arrive at a lower value we regard as safe; and where, in assessing consolidation settlement, we arrive at the *allowable* bearing capacity, which may be even lower still. Ideas on concrete mixes have advanced in the meantime, and the economics relating to the use of higher-strength steel reinforcements have changed. A new British Standard, BS 4461 (1969) (Amended 1970): *Cold-worked steel bars for the reinforcement of concrete,* has been published.

It is hoped that in all these ways the book is now up-to-date again, and that the elementary principles remain clear. If nothing more, the book should enable architects and those engineers not having the fullest knowledge of foundation matters to appreciate the problems likely to arise, to understand which parts of the work should be entrusted to a specialist, and to know what information and testing that specialist is likely to require.

The first edition of this book was written jointly with Frank Mead B.Sc., M.I.C.E., a close colleague and friend, who, six years ago, decided to move to New Zealand and set up a new way of life for himself there. This second edition has been prepared with Brian Johnson, M.A. M.I.C.E., with whom I have enjoyed working closely over more recent years and who is appropriately in touch with the latest engineering practices and units commonly used in Britain today.

Harpenden   John Faber
Herts
August 1974

Contents

1

First principles

1.1. This is a book about foundations, not about soil mechanics; nevertheless soil mechanics comes into it. This may seem such a surprising first statement that it is desirable to go on and elaborate the point a little further.

The purpose of a foundation is to enable some particular load to be supported on the ground in such a manner that the ground underneath is not over-stressed as a result. So we need to know the amount of the load, and the strength of the ground; and often it is easier to estimate the load more accurately than it is to assess the strength of the ground.

Here we have to remember that foundation design is concerned with the ground as we find it in nature; and unfortunately we find it is so variable that even in a lump of clay the size of a football, and supposedly uniform, parts of the material are likely to vary in physical properties as much as 50 per cent either side of the average. Bear in mind, also, that real geological strata vary within themselves in a manner far less predictable than in a simple lump of clay; and any tests we make on small soil samples represent only the conditions at some particular depths chosen by chance in certain boreholes. The conditions at other depths in these boreholes and at the millions of other positions where no boreholes are sunk are likely to vary yet further. Thus we must not lose sight of the fact that our best estimates of the strengths of natural grounds are generally likely to be in error by anything up to 100 per cent.

Until about 20 years ago, progress in understanding the strength and behaviour of soils had been allowed to fall far behind that of other materials such as timber, steel, and concrete. This is not surprising, because the study of soils is so very much more complex. But when pioneers in the subject of soil mechanics first showed the way towards a scientific approach, such great enthusiasm was shown (often excessive enthusiasm) that people were soon imagining that the uncertainties of soil in its natural form could be eliminated, and foundation

engineering could be treated as something precise. This is the great
danger of soil mechanics; it is quite wrong to take the results of tests
on samples from a limited number of boreholes and believe one can
know with any certainty that the ground is good for so many kilonewtons per square metre, no more and no less.

More recently, practical engineers have come back to the view that
experience and judgment still play the most important part in solving
the majority of foundation problems. Indeed one of the great lessons
that has come out of the further developments of soil mechanics is
precisely this: that the ground as we find it in nature does not readily
lend itself to much precise scientific calculation in foundation design.
Nevertheless, the study of soil mechanics has enabled us to understand
the behaviour of soil particles, the effects of pore-water pressure, and
similar fundamentals, so we are now better equipped to recognize
guide-lines of safety and risk and unacceptability; but, except in rather
special circumstances, it is more the *principles* of knowledge thrown
up by soil mechanics that we benefit from today rather than too much
intricate detail in terms of very precise measurements and calculations.

The foregoing is not intended to decry in any way the excellent
progress that has been achieved in sample-taking and laboratory-testing
techniques. But these techniques only go further to confirm the consistent irregularity of the ground upon which we have to construct
our real foundations, and they continue to remind us that the behaviour of soils in practice is unpredictable to such a degree that, no
matter how sophisticated and elaborate our methods of testing them
are, we shall never know exactly the true strength and settlement
characteristics of the ground on any particular site in the same sort of
way as we can almost guarantee our knowledge of the strength and
extension characteristics of a piece of steel used in the construction of
a bridge or a building.

1.2. At this point some general comments must be made on the SI
units used throughout this book. The SI units are basically metric in
style, and enjoy the simplicity of the decimal system. Nevertheless,
they vary in detail from the c.g.s. metric system, previously established
on the continent of Europe, which used the gram as its unit for mass.

The SI system takes the *kilogram* (kg) — 1000 grams — as the unit
for *mass*, and the *newton* (N) as the unit for *force*. One newton is the
force which, acting on a mass of one kilogram for one second, changes
the velocity of the mass by one metre per second. If a mass of one

kilogram is allowed to drop, its speed at the end of one second is 9·8 metres per second. Hence the force of gravity on 1 kg is 9·8 N. This means that the newton is such a small unit that for many engineering purposes we think more conveniently in terms of the *kilonewton* (kN) — 1000 N — as our practical minimum; and it is generally the kilonewton we shall be using as our unit throughout this book.

A mass of 1000 kg (1 000 000 g) is equal to 1 megagram (Mg) and this is popularly referred to as a *tonne* (t). A tonne is almost exactly equal to 2200 lb, and this is so close to the 2240 lb of the old Imperial ton that for all practical purpose we can reckon that

$$1 \text{ tonne (SI)} = 1 \text{ ton (Imperial)}.$$

Stresses in solid bodies — which include practical ground pressures in engineering terms — are normally expressed in *kilonewtons per square metre* (kN/m^2), and this is the unit adopted throughout this book. (The pascal (Pa), which is 1 N/m^2, has been deliberately avoided here.) Comparing units of stress between SI and the old Imperial system we have:

$$1 \text{ kN/m}^2 = 0·0093 \text{ tonf/ft}^2$$

$$= 0·01 \text{ tonf/ft}^2 \text{ (approximately)},$$

and in view of what was said previously in §1.1 about the imprecise nature of our understanding of ground strengths, it will be realized that the error of such an approximation is immaterial.

As we have now indicated the rough links between SI and Imperial units, the student should be able to retain a feel for comparisons wherever this may be desirable; henceforth the units used throughout the book will be in accordance with the SI.

1.3. Let us now consider a simple independent pad foundation for a reinforced-concrete column 300 mm × 300 mm, carrying a direct load of 500 kN. (Strictly speaking this is a *force* of 500 kN, and arises from the column supporting a *mass* of about 50 tonnes.) If this column were built directly on a thick stratum of sound granite, no harm would result; the pressure applied to the granite would be

$$\frac{500 \text{ kN}}{0·300 \text{ m} \times 0·300 \text{ m}} = 5540 \text{ kN/m}^2,$$

and this would be perfectly safe.

However, a 500 kN load on the same column built directly on a bed of medium clay would push the column through the clay and out of sight. This is because the clay, being very much softer than granite, cannot sustain the same pressure. A more suitable bearing pressure to allow on the clay would be 100 kN/m², so that a foundation would be required of plan area

$$\frac{500 \text{ kN}}{100 \text{ kN/m}^2} = 5 \text{ m}^2,$$

that is, about 2·25 m × 2·25 m. This is indicated in Fig. 1.1(a).

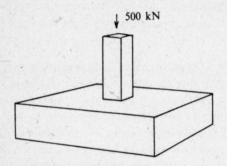

(a) Independent spread foundation

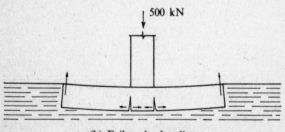

(b) Failure by bending

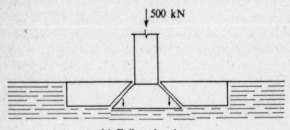

(c) Failure by shear

FIG. 1.1. Column spread foundation

With such a foundation, 2·25 m × 2·25 m, we know that, generally speaking, each part of the clay under the foundation must be supporting the underside of the foundation with a pressure of 100 kN/m². (If this were not so, clearly some parts of the clay would be pressing more and others less, because the total force from the ground must balance the total load from the column; and our design assumption is that the clay in question cannot press more than 100 kN/m².) We see, therefore, that the foundation is being pressed upwards from beneath over an area very much greater than the area of the column. In consequence, the foundation concrete has certain duties to perform. If it is too thin, it may break, either in bending (Fig. 1.1(b)) or by the column punching its way right through in shear (Fig. 1.1(c)).

Thus we see that foundation design is in two parts. First we have to decide on the *allowable bearing pressure* that the ground can safely sustain. This may vary from about 10 000 kN/m² for exceptionally sound rocks, to 25 kN/m² or less for silts and very soft clays. The allowable bearing pressure will determine the plan area of the foundation, and this will influence the thickness of concrete and amount of reinforcement required to ensure that the foundation is *strong enough* not to fail in bending or by shear.

Generally the greatest difficulty in foundation design is to decide on the correct bearing value to allow on the ground. If we are too conservative in our estimate, the cost of the foundations will become excessive. It is important, therefore, to know what information should be collected to avoid such extravagance and, having collected the information, we must know how it is to be interpreted.

One purpose of this book is to show how the allowable bearing pressures for various forms of stata can best be determined; and then how to design and calculate suitable foundations so that the ground pressures are limited to the allowable values.

1.4. Consider again our 300 mm × 300 mm column, loaded to 500 kN but supported on strata as shown in Fig. 1.2. The upper 5 m is clay, good for 100 kN/m², and beneath this is sound granite. Clearly there are two possible foundation arrangements: either we could excavate 5 m down and sit directly on the granite without any need to spread the load; or alternatively we could provide a foundation 2·25 m × 2·25 m higher up on the clay. The foundation on the clay will require more concrete and steel reinforcement but will entail less excavation

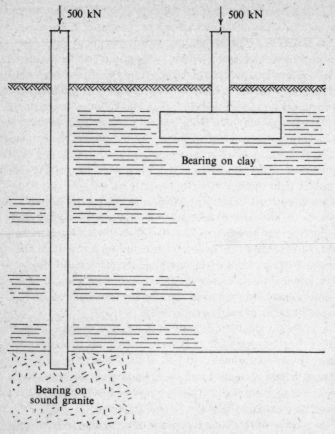

FIG. 1.2. Choice of foundation level

work. A number of considerations such as *time, convenience,* and *cost* will arise in settling the choice.

The example shown in Fig. 1.2 is fairly clear-cut. Generally the strength of the ground varies less markedly than from 100 kN/m² to 5000 kN/m², and the change may be spread over greater depths than 5 m. This indicates the need for exploratory boring work before it is possible to decide on the most suitable depth for founding in any given case.

1.5. Sometimes the soil for the upper part is good for less than 100 kN/m², and the depth to reach harder material may be greater than 5 m.

In this case it may be very costly to spread the load sufficiently in the upper soil; also the cost of excavating to the harder material may be prohibitive.

In these circumstances a foundation may be provided more cheaply by driving *piles* through the soft upper strata so as to reach and derive support from the harder strata below. Frequently conditions are such that bored piles are used instead of driven piles.

All these considerations will be discussed more fully in Chapter 7.

1.6. In the examples given in §§1.4, 1.5, and 1.7, the natural level at which the water stands in the ground — that is, the level of the *water table* — can have considerable influence on the decisions needing to be taken. Excavation below water-level is generally difficult and costly; furthermore, in certain circumstances the nature of the soil may be influenced by interference with its water conditions, resulting in a change in the soil's strength. This is touched upon further in subsequent chapters.

Buoyant foundation

1.7. Sometimes soft, silty ground is found extending to depths of 50 m or more. In such cases even piling may offer no practical solution, the piles pushing into the ground almost as easily at 50 m depths as at 5 m depth.

In these circumstances a *buoyant foundation* may be necessary. This, in essence, is like a ship floating on the water. According to Archimedes' principle, the buoyancy of a body immersed in a fluid is equal to the weight of the fluid it displaces. If a ship plus its contents weighs 10 000 tonnes, it must be lowered into the water so as to displace 10 000 tonnes of water before its downward weight is just balanced by the upward buoyancy: this is the level at which the ship will float.

The situation for a buoyant foundation is similar. Fig. 1.3 shows a hollow foundation 5 m deep (stiffened internally with cross-walls). This is very much lighter than the weight of ground it has been constructed to replace. Roughly, for every square metre of plan area, the 5 m depth of ground removed by excavation represents a relief of pressure on the soil of about $100 \, kN/m^2$, whereas the weight of the buoyant foundation itself is equivalent to only about $40 \, kN/m^2$, so that the net buoyancy effect is $(100 - 40) \, kN/m^2 = 60 \, kN/m^2$. This buoyancy effect can be set against a part of the downward pressure

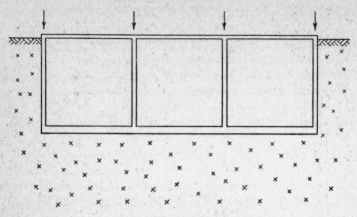

FIG. 1.3. Buoyant foundation

from the superstructure load, so as to relieve the *net loading intensity* applied to the soil.

Suppose the columns are arranged at 5 m centres in both directions as shown in Fig. 1.3, and each carry a load of 2500 kN. Then the gross downward loading intensity is

$$\frac{2500 \text{ kN}}{(5 \text{ m} \times 5 \text{ m})} = \qquad 100 \text{ kN/m}^2.$$

From this we can subtract the upward buoyancy effect of   60 kN/m².

This leaves us a *net loading intensity* on the soil of only   40 kN/m².

This may well be within the sustaining capacity of the silt.

Ground heave

1.8. A word of warning needs to be given about deep excavations in soft ground, as referred to in the previous example. The upward buoyancy effect is a natural tendency (resulting from the pressures from the ground remaining to the sides of the excavation) for the excavation bottom to rise. This phenomenon is known as *ground heave*, and if not properly watched out for and controlled can lead to much difficulty with the construction works.

Furthermore, once ground heave is allowed to occur, the relief of pressure which is relied upon in calculating the buoyancy effect will not become effective until the foundation has pressed the ground back to its original configuration. Thus it is important that the amount of ground heave should be controlled consistent with the amount of settlement that is acceptable for the foundation. This may well lead to problems which require much skill and experience on the part of the engineer.

2

Rocks and soils

2.1. Engineers classify the materials which form the outer layers of the world's surface broadly as *rocks* and *soils*. Rocks are hard, brittle masses, whereas soils consist of particles with water or air contained in the spaces between.

Rocks include granite, limestone, sandstone, marble, slate, and others; it is common knowledge that these materials are so hard, strong, and permanent that they give excellent service as building materials.

Soils, on the other hand, include such materials as clay, sand, and gravel. These are not suitable in their natural form as building materials, owing to porosity, impermanence, and their inability to stand to any height without support. However, clays may be baked dry to form bricks; and sands and gravels form excellent ingredients for artificial conglomerates (concrete) when suitably cemented together.

In terms of agriculture, the best soils are composed largely of organic matter of a peaty vegetable nature; such soils promote the growth of healthy crops. However, these soils are quite unsuitable for building on, because they allow considerable subsidence when loaded; the organic constituents decompose, and the water is squeezed out. Thus it is important, when we talk of soils in engineering, to be clear that we mean materials such as clays, silts, sands, and gravels. We are not referring to soils rich in vegetable matter such as would delight the farmer or horticulturist.

Rocks can stand unsupported to very considerable heights. In nature, the cliffs along the south coast of Sussex are a striking example; and in artificial form we see railway cuttings standing sheer 25 m or more. But if the student will pour dry salt from a container on to a table, he will find that, however carefully he does this, he cannot get the salt to stand more steeply than a certain maximum angle. This is known as the *natural angle of repose* of the material. Soils cannot stand more steeply than their natural angle of repose, so that railway cuttings are sloped back at about 1 in 2, or sometimes more, depending on the nature of the soil.

This natural angle of repose of a soil depends greatly on its water content. For example, a stiff clay will stand vertically when first exposed but if wetted sufficiently can become so soft as to resemble a paste or liquid slurry. And though sand will stand well when appropriately damp, it is limited to a natural angle of repose when dry; and poorly graded sands, when saturated, slump in the fashion of a fluid — quicksand. Our childhood experiments at the seaside will have demonstrated these effects.

In broad terms then, rocks are hard, strong, and generally reliable for building on. But soils are of an unrigid yielding nature, liable to move or give way when loaded, and are sensitive to external influences. It normally happens, therefore, that good foundations on rock need only be very much smaller than would be required on soils. However, as a point in favour of soils, rocks are very much more expensive to excavate, sometimes causing delay and difficulty.

Rocks

2.2. Rocks may be divided into three main groups, their classification depending on the conditions governing their formation. Thus we have (1) *igneous rocks,* (2) *sedimentary rocks,* and (3) *metamorphic rocks.*

The interior of the earth is so hot that everything there is molten. Outside this molten interior is a hard outer shell known as the earth's crust. Igneous rocks are the direct result of molten minerals from the earth's interior cooling down at the earth's crust. The best-known rocks in this group are *granite* and *basalt.*

Sedimentary rocks are composed of smallish particles, cemented together or compacted by the weight of overlying material. In the cases of *sandstone* and *shale* the initial particles are derived from the earlier disintegration and breakdown of other rocks. In the cases of *limestone* and *chalk* the particles are the bony remains of animals and other small creatures. The particles in each case are transported by water, wind, or gravity and deposited in horizontal layers, prior to being cemented together or compacted to form rock. The hardness of the rock depends on the cementing material and the degree of compaction. *Shale* is formed from clays. Under pressure the water is removed, and in the process the material becomes laminated. If lamination does not occur, the rock is known as *mudstone.*

Metamorphic rocks are formed by the action of heat and pressure on either igneous or sedimentary rocks, which causes a change in the original rock structure. *Slates* are derived from shales and possess rather special and characteristic cleavage (splitting) planes. *Schists* have grains running in parallel orientation and are thus very susceptible to shear failure and cleavage along the planes of the grain faces. The most commonly known schist is marble, which originates from limestone. *Gneisses* have a structure which alternates schistose layers with others in which the crystal orientation is less well defined, giving a branded texture. The grain sizes in this type of rock are also coarser. Gneisses are thus stronger than schists.

Rock formation

2.3. The layers in which rocks are formed are known as *beds,* and the plane surfaces which mark interruptions in the action of deposition are known as *bedding planes* (see Fig. 2.1). Bedding planes frequently become parting planes and are accentuated by the effects of weather.

FIG. 2.1. Rock bedding-planes

Roughly at right-angles to the bedding planes, fractures develop across the beds, owing to internal stresses set up during the cooling or drying-out of the rock or to external effects such as pressure or movement. These fractures are called *joints.*

During their history some rock beds have become subject to enormous forces within the earth's crust which have caused the various strata to become inclined or folded. As a result of this movement and stressing, the rock may have fractured, with one part of the strata sliding over the other. This type of fracture is known as a *fault* (see Fig. 2.2).

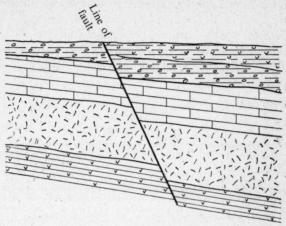

FIG. 2.2. Geological fault

Bearing capacity of rocks

2.4. While the unit strength of the material comprising the rock proper may be very considerable, the effective strength of a *rock formation* may be greatly influenced by the condition and inclination of the bedding planes and joints, and the position and complexity of any faults. For example, the actual limestone rock indicated in Fig. 2.3 may well be strong enough to support an applied pressure of 3000 kN/m^2; however, the safety of the formation here depends not on the strength of the limestone but on the slipperiness of the clay contained in the bedding planes. This clay will have entered the limestone by being washed down from above through a fault or through the joints,

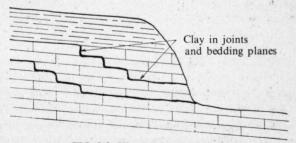

FIG. 2.3. Slip-planes in limestone

and the arrival of further water by the same route will probably lubricate the clay so as to leave little frictional resistance preventing the upper part of the limestone from sliding down to the right.

Thus, while the figures in Table 2.1 give *safe bearing capacities* for rocks evenly bedded and in sound condition, it is clear that it would be dangerous to work to these bearing values without first ensuring that the condition of the rock and the bedding planes is satisfactory. Where the strength of the rock itself is in doubt, specimen cores should be drilled out and tested.

TABLE 2.1
Safe bearing capacities of rocks

Type of rock	Safe bearing capacity (kN/m^2)
Igneous rocks and gneisses	5000 and more
Limestones and hard sandstones	Up to 3000
Schists and slates	Up to 2000
Shales and mudstones	Up to 1000
Hard block chalk	Up to 600

Certain rocks, particularly limestone, chalk, and shale, are liable to contain pot-holes, swallow-holes, or other solution channels. These can occur at all depths. St. Michael's Cave in the Rock of Gibraltar is an impressive example; the Cheddar caves are another. Smaller holes between 1 m and 5 m across can be sufficient to cause disaster to a local foundation, and it is wise to probe below the bottoms of foundation excavations to seek out such snares that lie in wait for the unwary.

Chalk, shales, and mudstones are liable to disintegrate on exposure to air and water, and for this reason the bottoms of the excavations in these materials should be covered as quickly as possible with a protective layer of concrete.

Formation of soils

2.5. Soils are formed by the disintegration of rocks. When water contained in joints or pores in a rock freezes, it does so with an increase in volume, and this has a wedging action, splitting the rock into smaller pieces. (This increase in volume is what causes pipes to burst in frosty weather.) Similarly, rain will wash away loose particles; and dilute acids dissolved in rainwater actually attack certain rocks. When rain gets into fissures and bedding planes, as shown in Fig. 2.3, it reduces frictional resistance, setting off landslides which result in shattered rock debris. Rivers and seas erode the rocks over which they flow and against which they wash.

Heat from the sun causes the breakdown of even the hardest rocks, because of alternating expansion and contraction. Where the minerals which form the rock have different coefficients of expansion, the rock structure itself breaks down with change of temperature.

Wind-blown and water-borne particles wear away rocks in much the same way as sandblasting is used to clean metallic surfaces.

All these processes lead to the breakdown of rocks into smaller particles of soil sizes. These are then carried by winds, rivers, seas, or ice sheets and deposited in beds of varying thicknesses over long periods of time (see Fig. 2.4). During these processes of transportation the particles are subjected to further abrasion and breakdown.

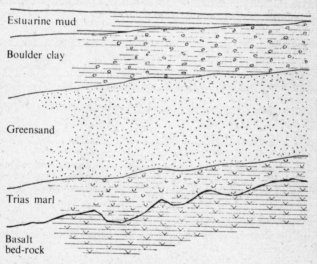

FIG. 2.4. Soil beds

Soil types

2.6. Soils are divided into groups according to their particle size. They range from boulders, gravels, sands, and silts down to clays. Often a particular stratum is made up of a mixture of these various soil types, so that in practice one meets 'sandy gravels', 'silty clays', and so on.

Soils rely for their strength on two physical properties. One is the property of *cohesion* — the attraction of small moist particles to one

another — the sort of gluey effect that causes clay to stick to your
boots. The other property is *frictional* — the roughness which prevents
adjacent particles from sliding freely past one another — much like the
roughness of two pieces of sandpaper being rubbed against one another.

For convenience, soils are classified according to whether or not
their strength is due mainly to cohesion. Thus we have *cohesive soils*
and *cohesionless soils.* Cohesionless soils derive their strength from
internal friction.

Cohesive soils have particles generally too small to be seen by the
naked eye; they include silts and clays. Cohesionless soils are of larger
particle size; these include sands, gravels, and boulders.

Fig. 2.5 indicates the proportions of particles of different sizes for
six typical soil samples. This manner of representing soil particle
sizes is standard and shows at a glance the range and proportion of
particle sizes in a given specimen, so that one can tell immediately
whether it is predominantly a silt or a sand or a clay and whether or
not the particle sizes are evenly graded.

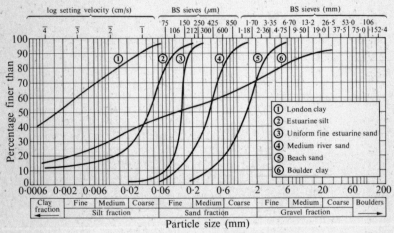

FIG. 2.5. Particle-size distribution curves

Soil behaviour

2.7. Cohesive soils (clays and silts) are compressed under load. This is
the effect of part of the internal water being squeezed out. The strength
of cohesive soils depends mainly on the particle sizes and on the surface
tensions in the water between the particles, which actually have the
effect of drawing the particles together. In simple terms, a uniform clay

will have a strength which is likely to remain roughly constant at all depths (except only above the level where seasonal effects like summer dryness and winter frost interfere).

Cohesionless soils (boulders, gravels, and sands), on the other hand, rely for their strength on the frictional effects of the individual particles resisting being rubbed past one another. This frictional strength depends on how the individual particles vary in size and shape, how they fit together, and how tightly they are packed.

When a cohesionless soil has little or no pressure applied to it, its strength is only small. This is like all other experiences of friction. An encyclopaedia will easily slide across the floor when no pressure is applied from above; but if someone stands his full weight on the book, the frictional force increases in proportion to the weight of the person, and the book becomes very much more difficult to move. Similarly, with cohesionless soils, the frictional strength increases roughly in proportion to the pressure applied, and we find that gravel and sand strata generally get stronger and stronger the deeper they are below the ground surface.

(Lack of cohesion is why it is so difficult to run over loose pebbles or very dry sand at the seaside – the sand is too weak to take the backward thrust from your feet, which slip backwards in consequence. Damp sand is not the same. This is because the moisture creates internal attractive forces (surface tensions) which give the sand some cohesive strength.)

Bearing capacity of soils

2.8. The matter of determining specific values for *safe bearing capacities* for soils is not easy. Tabulated values can often be misleading because similar soils vary from one another with no marked definition, and engineers often disagree on terms such as 'hard', 'stiff', and 'soft', as applied to clays, and 'compact', 'loose', and 'uniform', as applied to sands. This is all discussed at greater length in Chapters 3, 4, and 5. Nevertheless, Tables 2.2 and 2.3 are included here as giving a rough guide.

It will be seen later in the book that straightforward clays (cohesive soils) are relatively easy to sample and test in the laboratory, and readily lend themselves to calculation so far as safe bearing capacity is concerned. However, a very real problem then arises as to whether such cohesive soils will compress over a period of years and allow our foundation to settle, thus causing distress to the building or other superstructure supported on the foundation. It is because of this problem of consolidation settlement that foundations on clays often have to be designed for bearing pressures that are less than the *safe* bearing capacities. Such reduced bearing pressures are known as *allowable bearing pressures*.

TABLE 2.2
Safe bearing capacities for cohesive soils

Type of soil	Safe bearing capacity (kN/m²)
Very stiff clays and hard clays	300–600
Stiff clays	150–300
Firm clays	75–150
Soft clays and silts	Less than 75
Very soft clays and silts	Nil

Cohesive soils are susceptible to long-term consolidation as described in § 4.13. Whilst the bearing capacity figures given above are *safe*, it may nevertheless be necessary to work to *lower allowable bearing pressures*.

Later in the book we shall see that sands and gravels (cohesionless soils) are generally not convenient to sample, because they tend to spill and suffer undue disturbance. Such soils are therefore more usually tested *in situ* – generally in boreholes – and these testing techniques make an allowance in their interpretation of safe bearing capacities for likely settlement effects.

In CP 2004 (1972): *Code of practice for foundations,* qualitative guidance is given as to relative density of cohesionless soils, as follows. When examined in excavations, dense cohesionless soils offer a high resistance to penetration by a hand-bar. Some beds of gravel are so tightly packed that the material requires a pick for removal, and when struck may give a metallic ring. In the loose condition, cohesionless soils offer only a small resistance to penetration by a hand-bar and can easily be excavated with a shovel.

When cohesionless soils are *submerged,* the particles receive a hydrostatic buoyancy (like the buoyancy effect on a skin-diver), and this reduces the internal friction strength, roughly halving the bearing capacity of the soil. Therefore with foundations at ground level that are in or near the level of the ground-water, the safe bearing capacity should be taken as half the value for 'dry' conditions, and this is indicated in Table 2.3. Deeper submerged foundations do not need as much reduction as half, because of the 'ground heave' effect from the surrounding soil (see § 5.11).

Where the foundations in cohesionless soils are above ground-water level, but not sufficiently so to be classed as 'dry', intermediate values between 'submerged' and 'dry' may be taken in proportion.

A special situation arises in the case of sands having fine and uniform-sized particles occurring in a relatively loose state. When such sands are below the ground-water table they are familiarly known as *quicksands;* they run or blow when excavated. Normal pumping in such running sands presents some danger, since the water removed by pumping is liable to draw out with it many of the adjacent fine sand particles leading to ground subsidence and settlement of adjoining foundations. In such circumstances it may be necessary to support the sides of the excavations by the use of sheet piling or to make use of special de-watering techniques.

TABLE 2.3
Safe bearing capacities for cohesionless soils

Type of soil	Safe bearing capacity (kN/m²)	
	Dry	Submerged
Compact gravel and compact sandy gravel	600 and more	300 and more
Medium dense gravel and medium dense sandy gravel	200–600	100–300
Loose gravel and loose sandy gravel	Less than 200	Less than 100
Compact sand	300 and more	150 and more
Medium dense sand	100–300	50–150
Loose sand	Less than 100	Less than 50

The figures given above take into account reasonable settlement predictions related to the words 'compact', 'medium dense', and 'loose' as determined by penetration tests as described in § § 5.11 and 5.12.

Deposits composed of a mixture of different-sized particles, well graded, will tend to settle less than uniformly sized strata and the allowable bearing pressures will be correspondingly higher. This applies particularly with gravels and mixtures of sand and gravel.

'Dry foundations' are assumed to be above the highest ground-water level by an amount at least equal to the foundation breadth B.

Soil mechanics

2.9. The science known as 'soil mechanics' is intended to assist in determining truer values for safe bearing capacities for soils in specific cases; Chapters 4 and 5 are aimed at explaining how soil mechanics can best be used to this end. This science, used wisely, can give a better indication of soil strengths than the arbitrary reading of tables such as Table 2.2 or Table 2.3 or the casual prodding of a foundation bottom with the end of an umbrella.

But let us be clear that soil mechanics is not a cut-and-dried exact science. It can never tell you the exact bearing capacity of a real soil, because all real soils vary widely in their physical properties at every metre of depth and at each metre of length and breadth across the extent of any construction site. Soil mechanics can only tell you about the strength of a very small volume of soil at such-and-such depth in one of a few boreholes, and this sample may be either stronger or weaker than the ground only a few metres away, whether deeper or to one side or another.

No use, then, to bow down and worship soil mechanics. No use either to average the test results, which would be virtually as senseless as ignoring the poorer results — the weak links in the chain. We shall still need to apply intelligent judgement in knowing what to do with the findings of our tests, because soils in nature are so variable; so persistently variable, in fact, that no one true answer for an allowable bearing capacity could ever exist, and indeed, if any soil study pretended that the matter was simple and free from confusion, it would clearly be so insensitive a science as to be untrustworthy.

In Chapters 4 and 5 we shall see what soil mechanics has to offer — how we take samples from the ground, how we test them in the laboratory, and what the results mean when we get them. Then we shall work through some typical examples of foundation design to get some idea of the limits of accuracy necessary to enable us to choose one form of foundation rather than another. We shall find that often we have little need to work closely to the theoretical values for allow- able bearing capacities, and that the conception of the foundation anatomy affects the economy of the matter more than any precise mathematical calculation.

3

Site investigations

3.1. Suppose we have to design the foundations for a building on a site where we know the soil is consistent in character and extends without change for a considerable depth. If we have had experience of this sort of soil before, we may be able to judge from its feel and appearance how many kilonewtons per square metre it will safely carry. For example, you can push the blunt end of a pencil quite easily into a softish clay which will bear about $100 \, kN/m^2$; it requires a good firm pressure to get the pencil into a $200 \, kN/m^2$ clay; and you will have great difficulty in getting the pencil into a $400 \, kN/m^2$ clay at all.

But these rule-of-thumb methods can mean very little to people without a good deal of experience behind them. It is only when you have dealt with a number of clays that you can have any confidence in judging the strength of others by comparison. Even then it is easy to be misled, and such methods are, at best, only very approximate.

3.2. There are on the market a number of devices rather more scientific than just pushing a pencil into the clay. For example, the *pocket penetrometer-gauge* consists of a protruding steel rod – rather similar to our pencil – which activates a spring balance operating a small gauge calibrated to give directly the bearing pressure in kilonewtons per square metre when the rod is pressed steadily and held firmly in the clay.

The Serota *pocket shear-vane* has a cruciform vane (19 mm across) on the end of a similar rod. The vane is pushed into clay and rotated at a constant rate of one revolution per minute – easily checked against the second hand of a watch. The rod acts upon a helical spring which operates a pointer callibrated to give directly the cohesive strength of the clay.

Trial pits

3.3. A satisfactory way of seeing the nature of the strata below ground level is to dig a number of trial pits. This enables the simple prodding or shear-vane tests just described to be made at various levels. By lining the pits with open timbering the soil can be seen in its virgin state, and a good general impression of the extent of variation obtained. Samples can be taken as required and kept for qualitative examination, or for testing as described later in Chapter 5.

Reference has been made earlier to the significance of water in soils. Sands and clays stand differently depending on whether they are dry or wet, and the safe bearing pressures on cohesionless soils are much influenced by how close they are to the ground-water table. The ease or difficulty of excavation work is also much affected by the presence or absence of water. Accordingly, it is important to make a note of the level at which water is first reached in our trial pits, and if the water-level is found subsequently to rise a note should also be made of this. Any seasonal or tidal variations should be noted too.

A special merit of ground examination by trial pits is that it gives a feel of the practical problems of opening up the ground. Nothing is as convincing to an engineer as to see how the sides of an excavation actually stand or crumble or collapse. The ease with which the excavation sides and bottoms can be trimmed gives a useful indication of the accuracy to which it is worth working in the foundation design, and also the likely trouble and cost it will be subsequently to make the actual full-size excavations.

On the site of a modest-sized building, a fair impression of the ground conditions might well be achieved from only two or three trial pits, provided foundation pressures are not going to be too ambitious. For a more extensive development, such as a low-rise housing complex occupying several hectares, it might be suitable to have trial pits spaced at about 30 m intervals, unless preliminary pits at the corners of the site indicate considerable uniformity, in which case it may suffice to double that spacing.

It generally becomes expensive to dig trial pits more than about 5 m deep, and below this depth it is more usual to make borings. For projects of major engineering significance it is normal to undertake a general borehole study, although sometimes this is followed with a number of trial pits to give a feel of practical conditions down to foundation level.

Shallow boreholes

3.4. In unconsolidated soils, shallow borings can be made with hand-augers. These are worked either from ground level, or sometimes from the bottoms of trial pits. Trial pits need to be a little larger than would otherwise be required if borings are to be made from the bottom. It is not normal to line the holes of auger borings with steel casings. Such boreholes are usually limited to about 5 m penetration.

For investigations to greater depths, and wherever waterlogged soils are encountered, the boreholes are cased with sectional steel tubing. Boring is then carried out as described in § 3.5. Generally these boreholes are made 150 mm diameter.

'Shell-and-auger' boring

3.5. Boreholes in this country are most frequently made by what is known as *percussion boring*. This omnibus term covers the use of *percussion chisels, clay cutters, augers,* and *shell 'balers'*. These tool-

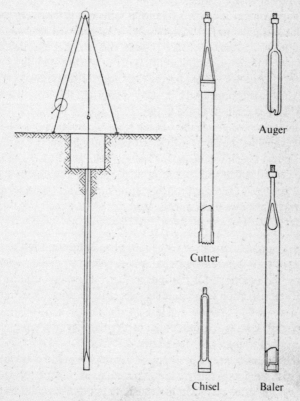

Auger

Cutter

Chisel   Baler

FIG. 3.1. Shell-and-auger boring gear

attachments are all operated from ground level, using a simple four-legged derrick fitted with a winch — the whole assembly being known collectively as the *'shell-and-auger gear'*. The tool-attachments are illustrated in Fig. 3.1.

Percussion chisels, suitably weighted, are repeatedly dropped in the borehole so as to break up the soil. The debris is then lifted from the bottom of the hole using the *shell baler*. This is fitted with a simple flap valve (much like a force-pump), and by repeatedly dropping the shell the debris passes up through the valve until the chamber is full. The shell is then lifted out of the hole, and the debris is recovered at ground level.

Percussion chisels are used mainly for boring in compact sands, gravels, and chalk. The shell (without the chisel) operates satisfactorily in wet sands or blowing soils.

For boring in dry sands or silt, and in some clays, the *auger* tool is used. This is rotated in the borehole on a steel rod, and acts very much like the bit on a carpenter's brace-and-bit, the spoil being collected internally within the tool instead of falling to waste externally.

The *clay cutter* is used for boring firm clays. The tooth-edged open-ended cylinder is dropped into the clay, and when this is pulled out again the clay is retained in the cutter.

The material brought to the surface from the boreholes is carefully recorded, showing the different types and depths below the surface, the thickness of each soil or rock layer, the level at which water is struck, and the level to which this rises after being left for a period to stand. Selected samples of the soil brought to the surface are carefully stored and labelled for subsequent examination.

3.6. Where boreholes are used to provide general information to classify the types of soils to be encountered, their spacing would be generally similar to that described for trial pits in § 3.3. However, where quantitive information is required in association with soil-mechanics tests as described in Chapter 5, a more sophisticated approach is probably desirable, as it is likely that somewhat higher bearing pressures will be worked to under the foundations.

In such circumstances a programme of attack would be drawn up, starting with boreholes fairly widely spaced, so as to get a feel for the likely variation of strata. Then intermediate boreholes would be put down based on the evidence of the earlier ones. There should never be less than three boreholes on any but the most trivial of jobs, otherwise one cannot hope to detect any variation or slope of strata.

Such boreholes should normally be taken down far enough to give evidence of the strata at a depth $1\frac{1}{2}$–2 times the plan dimension of the foundations. This is true at any rate until the general pattern of the strata has been understood. Subsequent intermediate boreholes giving supplementary information about any local variations may not need to keep proving the deeper-lying material. The logic of all this is clear from § 4.14, and from Figs 4.6 and 4.8. Where the sizes and pressures under foundations are such that significant stress occurs in the ground as the spread from adjacent foundations overlaps, the boreholes need to be taken down somewhere near twice the plan dimension of the total structure.

Thus for a pad foundation 3 m square, until the characteristics of the site have been understood, boring should go down to a depth approaching 6 m. However, for larger structures, where the influence of adjacent foundations overlaps, or where a raft foundation is used, it will be necessary to explore far deeper. For example, a heavy industrial structure 12 m wide might require soil examination to a depth of about 18 m or 24 m, unless rock were struck at some lesser depth or local knowledge or records indicated improved strata at increasing depths.

Weaker soils may be permissible at greater depths – provided we *know* of their existence and *satisfy ourselves* that they are adequate for the reduced applied stresses to which they will be subject.

It is quite normal for boreholes to be spaced across a medium-sized site at about 35 m intervals. On smaller jobs – including modest buildings – where the boreholes are not likely to be very deep, a spacing of 20 m is common. For very large projects a borehole spacing as much as 70 m may suffice, with intermediate boreholes being placed to pick up suspected local variations, or where unusual or critical loads are likely to come.

3.7. Where only *qualitative* information is being obtained, as from trial pits and the simple baler and auger tools shown in Fig. 3.1, it is a reasonable return for a relatively modest cost that the sample material we collect for inspection is *disturbed*. It gives us a general indication of the nature of the underlying strata at various depths.

For example, the presence of a layer of compressible peat, 10 m down, would guide an engineer immediately as to the form of foundation he should adopt (and certainly what form of foundation he should avoid!). And the knowledge that a soft clay layer underneath what had looked like a good reliable sand would give an immediate warning. And so on.

However, these disturbed samples are unsuitable as a basis for carrying out any scientific strength-tests in a laboratory. In Chapter 5 we shall consider the problem of how we are to obtain *undisturbed samples* of the soils encountered in our boreholes. But let the reader first bear patiently with the present chapter, since too much enthusiasm for the work of Chapter 5 — particularly when it is taken out of context — can do as much to mislead the unwary as to help. The first essential is to form a good general commonsense impression of the overall conditions on any construction site; this is worth any number of suspect laboratory tests, and can generally be done more quickly and at considerably less cost. The authors regard the following simple procedures as quite essential.

In the first place, the engineer responsible for the design work should visit the site and involve himself personally in the investigation. He should walk over the ground, looking for any curious features such as rock outcrops, sudden variations of level, soft spots, marsh, springs, flooding, or the like. He should also walk about the areas which surround the site, since this often throws up useful information in the form of quarry workings, streams, or other construction sites. All these observations should be carefully recorded and mapped.

The engineer should then concern himself with the siting of the various trial pits and boreholes, and be present to examine the sides and bottoms of the pits and see the material from the boreholes when it is actually being brought up. Soils change in nature and colour very rapidly on exposure to the air, and it is quite misleading to judge the virgin conditions by looking at dried-out samples, or — worse still — to gain one's information second or third hand, from a chargehand's notes which have subsequently been edited and typed in someone else's office.

Perhaps the most vital points for the engineer to watch out for and record from the trial pits and boreholes are

(1) colour
(2) consistency
(3) particle size
(4) water-level.

These all need assessing most carefully, and recording as to position on site, depth below measured ground level, and date. It is only from such detailed personal records that the engineer will be able to study realistically the characteristics of the site on which his design decisions will have to be made. And it is only from such exercises that the student will ever be able to gain the true experience he will require for use in later years.

Colours should be recorded in simple terms of red, orange, or yellow (for the bright ones), and brown, olive-green, or blue (for the darker ones). Then from borehole to borehole it is likely that the variation and slope of the various strata will be detectable.

So far as *consistency* is concerned, Tables 3.1 and 3.2 offer a practical basis for comparisons which should help take a little of the uncertainty out of descriptive terminology that otherwise tends to suffer from the drawback of being only relative. These two tables are adapted from the collection of experience by Jennings.

TABLE 3.1
Field indications of consistency for cohesive soils

Description	Consistency
Very stiff or hard	Very tough and difficult to move with hand-pick; requires pneumatic spade for excavation
Stiff	Cannot be moulded in fingers; cannot be cut with hand-spade, and requires hand-picking for excavation
Firm	Can be moulded in the fingers by strong pressure; difficult to cut with hand-spade
Soft	Easily moulded in the fingers; heelmarks show
Very soft	Exudes between the fingers when squeezed in the fist

Particle size serves not only as a means of classification; it also gives an immediate indication of drainage characteristics. Gravels and clean sands are generally free-draining, whereas silts and clays normally drain

TABLE 3.2
Field indications of consistency for cohesionless soils

Description	Consistency
Compact	High resistance to picking; requires pneumatic tools for excavation
Dense	Very high resistance to penetration by hand bar; requires hand-pick for excavation
Medium dense	Considerable resistance to shovelling or penetration by hand-bar
Loose	Small resistance to shovelling or penetration by hand-bar
Very loose	Very easily excavated with hand-spade

extremely slowly, if at all. Particles larger than 60 mm are generally reckoned as boulders; from 60 mm to 2 mm are classified as gravel; and material from 2 mm down, still clearly visible to the eye, can be taken as sand. Silts have particles of size generally not visible, but feel gritty in the hand; clays are so fine that, when rubbed with water in the hand, they feel soapy.

Many sections of this book discuss the major significance of *water-levels* in the ground, yet it is surprising how often people get caught out in foundation work as a result of failure to collect and record properly the vital evidence necessary on this one basic point. In bore-holes, a record should be made of the level at which water is first struck; and if subsequently the level rises, a record should be made of the rate of rise and the highest level reached. Seasonal variations of water-level are not infrequent, and a check can be made on this quite. simply by setting a stand-pipe with its lower end in gravel near the bottom of the borehole and then grouting the remainder of the hole up to ground level.

Loading tests

3.8. Some grounds do not lend themselves readily to the collection of samples for testing in the laboratory. Sands and gravels loosen and spill, and are assessed differently by penetration tests as described in

§§ 5.11 and 5.12. Gravels of cobble sizes, however, cannot be tested by penetration methods, and recourse must then be made to plate-bearing tests. Certain soft rocks, too, such as chalk, shale, and keuper marl, are frequently more conveniently tested *in situ* by direct loading tests.

It is also useful sometimes to test-load certain clays, for example, those that contain angular fragments; such clays often develop hair-cracks, and because of this are liable to disintegrate in the process of making up into laboratory test specimens. Loading tests in the case of clays are less popular than they were 10 or 20 years ago; nevertheless it will be of interest to examine the procedure for such a test since it brings out clearly the features of behaviour of any softish ground material under load.

If we expect that our foundations are going to be, say, 1·5 m below ground level, this will be the level for making our test. We dig a hole 1·5 m deep, trim the bottom to a level, even surface, and place on it a concrete or steel pad of some definite size. A suitable size for a pad in the case of a clay is 0·40 m², which is 635 mm × 635 mm. Larger pads require such large test loads as to be rather inconvenient; and smaller pads on clay are too susceptible to local variations or weaknesses in the ground and, apart from giving misleading results, are inclined to tilt and behave awkwardly. However, smaller pads are often used on sandy soils.

3.9. Let us consider the details of an actual loading test carried out on a firm clay. A concrete pad 635 mm × 635 mm was cast directly on the clay, and the load was applied using a hydraulic jack pressing against the underside of steel beams supporting about 200 kN of steel billets (see Fig. 3.2).

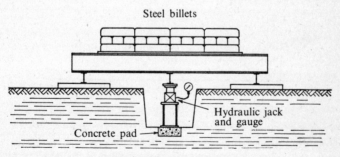

FIG. 3.2. Ground loading test

The jack was pumped to 20 kN, and maintained at this load for 24 hours. The amount the concrete pad settled was recorded, first just after the 20 kN load was applied and again at the end of the 24 hours. In this case a dial gauge was used for measuring the settlements, though some engineers are content with the accuracy obtained by using a surveyor's level.

The 20 kN spread over the area 0·40 m² gave an applied pressure on the clay of

$$\frac{20 \text{ kN}}{0·40 \text{ m}^2} = 50 \text{ kN/m}^2,$$

and at this pressure the immediate settlement was 0·66 mm; the settlement after 24 hours was 0·79 mm — not a very material increase.

Next, the jack was pumped to 40 kN, giving an applied pressure of

$$\frac{40 \text{ kN}}{0·40 \text{ m}^2} = 100 \text{ kN/m}^2,$$

and once more the settlement was measured immediately and again after a further 24 hours. And so the process was repeated, stage by stage, until the total load applied was 160 kN — equivalent to a pressure of 400 kN/m². The total settlement was then 31·38 mm.

The results of the tests are indicated in Table 3.3.

TABLE 3.3

Applied load (kN)	Pressure (kN/m²)	Settlement (mm)	
		Immediate	After 24 hours
20	50	0·66	0·79
40	100	1·55	2·08
60	150	2·97	3·56
80	200	4·52	5·47
100	250	7·28	8·12
120	300	10·63	14·82
140	350	18·58	22·80
160	400	27·50	31·38

The same results are also indicated graphically in Fig. 3.3. The dotted curve is made up of a series of kinks, each representing the sudden increase in settlement that occurred immediately after each load increment, followed by a period of relative lull until the time of the

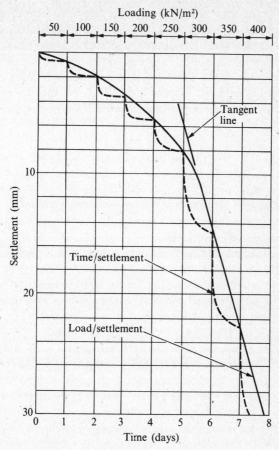

FIG. 3.3. Settlement curves of loading test

next load increment. The full-line curve in Fig. 3.3 is drawn through the points of maximum settlement occurring after the 24-hour rest periods, and this curve represents the relationship between load and final settlement for our 0·40 m² test pad. (It is not strictly true that the settlement after a 24-hour period would be *final*, though for our purpose and with a test as elementary as we are describing here, the settlement can be regarded as near-enough final.)

Load—settlement graphs of this type vary in form according to the nature of the soil. Dense or stiff soils show a sudden increase of settlement once the *ultimate bearing capacity* has been exceeded. Loose or softer soils, on the other hand, display no sudden failure and the curve gradually bends over little by little; in such cases the failure load is taken as the point where the slope of the curve becomes more pronounced.

In the case of the graph shown in Fig. 3.3 the *ultimate bearing capacity* would be regarded as about $300 \, \text{kN/m}^2$, and the *allowable bearing pressure* would be somewhere between $100 \, \text{kN/m}^2$ and $150 \, \text{kN/m}^2$.

3.10. Some people decry the very idea of loading tests on soils, and will argue that a test on a small pad is so limited in application as to be useless or even misleading. These scientifically minded people prefer, curiously, to rely on the results of tests on very much smaller laboratory samples as against the volume of soil influenced by a test load, say, 0·75 m across and about 1 m deep.

When we remember that the loading test deals with the soil *in situ*, with the moisture content and adjoining soil reactions exactly as they would be for the full-size foundation, it is difficult to share this greater enthusiasm for tests on small samples (necessarily disturbed, though reputedly not) which may with luck be typical of the strata they represent but, more probably, are either better or worse.

Certainly for *simple* site investigations there is a lot to be said in favour of the loading test. It is a relatively cheap operation to conduct, and for works of not too ambitious a scale, where the ground is reasonably uniform, it still takes a lot of beating. If the limitations of the method are properly appreciated, there may be less likelihood of error than with the more scientific methods described in the chapters that follow.

The limitations of loading tests

3.11. Now loading tests, as described above, are satisfactory when we know the soil is uniform in character and extends without change over an adequate depth. We can determine whether this is so by the simple methods described in §§ 3.3–3.7.

Where the ground varies at greater depths, the danger of relying only on the results of loading tests is illustrated in Fig. 3.4. Clearly, within the soil the influence of loading a small test pad will be relatively local, whereas the effect of loading a larger structure will extend much further. Thus a loading test may indicate only the

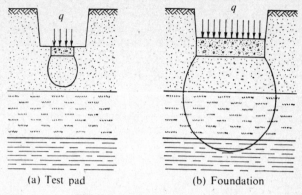

(a) Test pad   (b) Foundation

FIG. 3.4. Limitation of loading test

strength of an upper crust or hard layer, whereas a heavy structure will
need to rely on the strengths of the soil layers at far greater depths.

Settlement of foundations

3.12. Accurate *settlement* calculations are difficult to make, and are
often of uncertain validity; but if we revert to our loading test described
in § 3.9 we can get a very good idea of the likely settlement of a full-
size foundation on fairly uniform strata — probably sufficient for many
everyday problems.

On cohesive soils, the settlement of rectangular foundations is
roughly proportional to the breadth of the foundation. Thus, in the
case of the test already described, if we decide to work to a bearing
pressure on the clay of 150 kN/m², we know that the settlement of
our square pad of 0·635 m side is 3·56 mm; and if our actual foundation works out to be 2 m square, we can anticipate a settlement of
about

$$3\cdot56 \text{ mm} \times \frac{2\cdot000}{0\cdot635} = 11\cdot2 \text{ mm}.$$

With cohesionless soils (sandy soils) the relationship between settlement and foundation breadth is not so simple. A useful size for a test
pad on sand is 0·10 m², given by a square 317 mm × 317 mm. An
approximate formula in these circumstances intended for foundations
on homogeneous sand is

$$\Delta = \Delta_1 \left(\frac{2B}{B + 0\cdot317} \right)^2, \tag{3.1}$$

where Δ is the settlement of a foundation of breadth B and Δ_1 is the settlement of a test pad $0 \cdot 317$ m square under the same intensity of loading. For example, suppose a test pad $0 \cdot 317$ m square had settled $2 \cdot 5$ mm under the same pressure as that decided on for the design of a full-size foundation. Then the settlement of a foundation 2 m square would be

$$\Delta = 2 \cdot 5 \left(\frac{2 \times 2 \cdot 000}{2 \cdot 000 + 0 \cdot 317} \right)^2 \text{ mm}$$

$$= 7 \cdot 5 \text{ mm.}$$

4

Theory of soil behaviour

4.1. In Chapter 2 we saw that soils are made up of particles of different sizes — clays being of very small particle size, and sands and gravels being of much larger particle sizes. The other ingredient that occurs in all soils in varying degrees is water, and the significance of this is referred to further in §4.4.

In simple terms, soils can be regarded as relying for their strength on two physical properties — *cohesion* and *friction*. True clays are cohesive — sticky, while not gritty; dry sands are frictional — the particles grate against one another, but have no stickiness.

A pure scientist would argue that even in clays quite a proportion of the soil strength resides in friction between the very small particles, and that the material holds together because of surface tensions developed in the pore-water occupying the spaces between the particles. Indeed it can be argued that it is the pulling-together of the particles by the pore-water tensions that helps achieve the frictional contact between the particles. This matter of pore-water behaviour is discussed in §4.4. Nevertheless, for our present purpose, we need not concern ourselves with such academic study. The important thing is to be clear that in soils of small particle size — mainly clays — the strength from the combined effects of friction and pore-water tensions is *what we call cohesion*.

It is possible to express the properties of cohesion and friction in the form of a mathematical equation, and there are two good reasons for doing this.

First, it enables us to describe the total strength of any given soil specifically in terms of its cohesive and frictional properties. It would be clumsy if we had to describe a silty clay having both cohesive and frictional properties as being so much per cent cohesive plus so much per cent frictional. Indeed the frictional strength of a soil varies according to the pressure at the depth considered (see §2.7), so that the contribution of the friction to the total strength of the soil varies according to the loading and to the depth. These matters are all conveniently taken care of by the use of our one mathematical equation.

The second advantage of expressing the properties of our soil by a mathematical equation is the following. The tests we are able to make in the laboratory give us results which require a certain amount of manipulation before we can separate (for calculation purposes) the share of the strength which is due to the cohesion from the share which is due to friction. Once we have achieved in our minds this idea of separating artificially the cohesion from the friction, it becomes quite simple to calculate the strengths of soils in all normal situations. Of course, one cannot in practice take a silty clay and separate the cohesion from the friction in the same way as one can take a nut and separate the shell from the kernel; but *mathematically* we can separate the two, and this is very convenient.

4.2. Fig. 4.1(a) shows the simplest way in which a foundation can fail. The diagram does not show the whole of the truth, but it shows a very

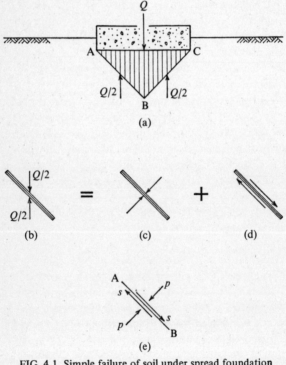

FIG. 4.1. Simple failure of soil under spread foundation

important part of it. The foundation pushes beneath itself a triangular-shaped wedge of soil, in much the same fashion as a simple snow-plough will push a triangle of snow in front of itself. Thus the soil particles within the triangle move down relative to the soil particles immediately outside the boundaries of the triangle. The only reactions which prevent the foundation and the triangle of soil from sinking further are the two forces $Q/2$.

Suppose we replace the boundary plane AB of the moving wedge with an imaginary piece of plywood. It is clear that part of the effect of $Q/2$ will be to squeeze or compress the plywood as at Fig. 4.1(c); and the other effect of $Q/2$ will be to try and slide the plys of the wood past one another as indicated at Fig. 4.1(d). If we now remove our imaginary piece of plywood, it is clear that the same forces must be acting as between the soil particles which lie on either side of the boundary plane AB.

The sliding effect indicated at Fig. 4.1(d) is known as *shearing*. (We take advantage of the same action in the garden when we cut the grass with 'shears', one blade of the shears sliding past the other and shearing the grass). The natural strength of a soil which acts to avoid failure of this kind is known as the *shear strength* of the soil. The shearing resistance of the soil is indicated at Fig. 4.1(e) by the arrows marked s.

The effect of squeezing or compression shown at Fig. 4.1(c) is also indicated at 4.1(e) by the arrows marked p. This is the total normal pressure across the shear plane.

When the soil fails under real foundations, the mode of soil failure is more complicated than indicated by the simple triangle at Fig. 4.1(a) (as will be discussed further in §§4.6 *et seq*.); nevertheless the principle we have established that the failure of the ground arises from a *shear failure of the soil* is entirely correct. Satisfactory foundations have to be designed so that the *shear stresses* in the soil are kept everywhere within limits that the soil can safely sustain.

Coulomb's equation

4.3. The shear strength of a soil is made up partly of cohesion and partly of friction. Let us denote these by the following symbols:

s = the shearing resistance of the soil,
c = the cohesion of the soil,
ϕ = the angle of internal friction of the soil,
p = the total normal pressure across the shear plane.

Then we can express the shearing resistance of the soil by the mathematical equation

$$s = c + p \tan \phi. \tag{4.1}$$

This equation was first put forward by Coulomb; it is perfectly simple in its meaning, and perfectly simple in its method of use. First let us understand its meaning.

Returning to Fig. 4.1, if our foundation had been sitting on a plastic clay, the whole of the support from the soil would have been due to what we have agreed to call cohesion. Then the total shear strength of the soil would have been equal to the cohesion; so that for a cohesive soil

$$s = c. \tag{4.2}$$

In other words, the $p \tan \phi$ of eqn. (4.1), which relates to friction, is equal to zero.

Suppose, on the other hand, our foundation had been sitting on dry sand. Then there would have been no cohesive strength, so that in eqn. (4.1) we have c equal to zero; and for a frictional soil

$$s = p \tan \phi. \tag{4.3}$$

Now ϕ is the angle of internal friction of the soil, and for a dry sand this has the same numerical value as its natural angle of repose. And p is the pressure across the plane of sliding (compare the analogy in §2.7 of the encyclopaedia sliding across the floor). Thus the greater the friction ϕ, the greater the shear strength, so that sharp angular particles give a stronger soil than a heap of ball-bearings, which would tend to slump or collapse. And the tighter the particles are wedged together by the pressure normal to the shear plane, the more difficult it is for the particles to slide past one another, and so, again, the stronger will be the soil.

Many soils are neither solely cohesive nor solely frictional. They rely for their strength on a mixture of both. We have already referred to silty clay as an example. Here the strength of the soil is due partly to cohesion and partly to friction, and the total shearing resistance of such a soil is given by the whole of eqn. (4.1), namely,

$$s = c + p \tan \phi.$$

This general equation may be used as follows. Suppose the cohesive strength of a soil is $100 \, \text{kN/m}^2$, the angle of internal friction is $25°$,

and the total normal pressure across the shear plane is $150 \, kN/m^2$; that is, $c = 100 \, kN/m^2$, $\phi = 25°$, and $p = 150 \, kN/m^2$.
Then

$$s \ = \ 100 + (150 \times \tan 25°).$$

We find $\tan 25°$ by looking up in a book of mathematical tables the natural tangent of $25°$, where we find $\tan 25° = 0\cdot466$. Therefore

$$s \ = \ 100 + (150 \times 0\cdot466) \, kN/m^2$$
$$= \ 100 + 70 \, kN/m^2$$
$$= \ 170 \, kN/m^2.$$

This value of $170 \, kN/m^2$ is the resistance of the soil to failure in the manner indicated in Fig. 4.1, with the triangular wedge of soil shearing its way down past the supporting soil. If we know how many kilonewtons load from our structure we have to support and how many square metres there are at the boundary plane of our triangular wedge, then we can work out whether the applied shear stress from the structure is greater than the shear strength of our soil. If, in our particular case, the shear stress resulting from the applied load is greater than $170 \, kN/m^2$, the soil will fail in shear and the foundation will sink. On the other hand, if the shear stress is less than $170 \, kN/m^2$, the soil will not fail.

In practice we allow some factor to give ourselves a margin of safety to cover many uncertainties, such as the variability of the soil and the inexactness of our calculations for the loading. We also work the problem in rather a different manner, as will be seen later in this chapter. But the elementary principles given above are fundamental, and if the reader has understood our aim in expressing the strength of the soil by Coulomb's equation, then the basis of soil mechanics will have been grasped.

In the foregoing numerical example we have tacitly assumed that the values of c, p, and ϕ were available to us. Indeed, such values can be determined by scientific tests which will be described in Chapter 5. However, before we learn how these values are obtained it is necessary to know more of how soils actually fail under foundations (more than Fig. 4.1) and what factors we should allow to give us reasonable margins of safety. The remainder of the present chapter is devoted to these matters.

We shall return to Coulomb's equation again at the beginning of Chapter 5, where we discuss the measurements of c and ϕ, and also in Chapter 8, where we deal with the pressures occurring at the faces of retaining walls.

4.4 When the student comes to read any of the literature that specializes in soil mechanics, he will find eqn. (4.1) sometimes written as

$$s = c + (p - u_w) \tan \phi, \qquad (4.4)$$

where u_w is the pore-water pressure (see below). This equation is more strictly correct. Nevertheless, bearing in mind the warnings given at appropriate stages throughout this book, the complication of eqn. (4.4) will be deliberately avoided. However, a brief explanation now follows, so that the reader may be aware of the meaning and significance of the term u_w.

In Britain and in many other countries where the water table is close enough, in engineering terms, to the surface of the ground to come within the levels at which the shear stresses from foundations are significant, the water gets between the solid particles of the soil and provides a hydrostatic buoyancy. The total normal pressure p at any level in the soil is then reduced by the pressure of the water — known as the *pore-water pressure* u_w — so that the *effective pressure* $\bar{p}$ is given by

$$\bar{p} = p - u_w. \qquad (4.5)$$

In any extended study of soil mechanics this equation has an important influence, as will now be explained.

In a dense soil where the particles are arranged and packed tightly against one another — what is known as a *dilatant particle structure* — when the soil is disturbed by a shear strain the particles take up more volume, with the result that the ratio of voids to particles increases and the pore-water pressure consequently drops. The exact reverse occurs in a loose soil, where a shear strain has the effect of collapsing the particle structure, causing the voids ratio to decrease, with a consequent increase in the pore-water pressure.

With permeable soils like coarse sands and gravels, the pore-water pressure changes are able to adjust themselves easily and rapidly; but with impermeable soils like silts and clays the adjustments can only take place very much more slowly.

For the purpose of the present discussion, clays can be considered in two types: *over-consolidated* clays and *normally-consolidated* clays.

An over-consolidated clay is one which at some stage has had part of its *overburden* (pressure from above) removed, so that it is consolidated to a degree greater than is compatible with its existing overburden. When such an over-consolidated clay is disturbed by a shear strain as described above, causing its pore-water pressure to decrease, it tends to suck in additional water, which causes softening of the material by interfering with the soil particles acting directly upon one another. Normally-consolidated clays, on the other hand, by virtue of their increase in pore-water pressure under strain, slowly exude water and actually get stronger in time under the effect of load.

Changes in strength resulting from shear strains in normally-consolidated clays are therefore not a source of worry to design engineers, since the clays only become stronger with time. With over-consolidated clays the position is not so comforting, as the material tends to develop weaknesses along its critical shear planes. However, in terms of foundation design, the quick undrained tests (as described in Chapter 5) fortunately give results that are safe to use, since these results relate in the first place to the immediate undrained condition; and subsequently — as vertical pressures are applied from above — the excess pore pressures dissipate and the friction between the soil particles is given the chance to increase its grip.

In the cases of engineering problems involving clays in natural and man-made slopes where no external forces exist to drive out the pore-water in this way, a very different situation can arise over lengthy periods of time, and more elaborate *slow drained tests* then become necessary to understand the fuller effects of eqn. (4.5). This is not a matter that needs concern us in our studies in the present book.

With permeable frictional materials like sands and gravels, the buoyancy effect of water within the relevant shear stress zones is highly significant; this is discussed in §2.8 in connection with cohesionless soils and again in §5.11 when we come to interpreting the results of standard penetration tests and Dutch cone tests.

Having said all this, the reader will now be aware of the effects of pore-water pressure; but, by the use of *quick undrained tests* on impermeable soils and with an appreciation of the significance of buoyancy on the strength of permeable soils, we can proceed further with our understanding of soil behaviour on the basis of the simple form of Coulomb's equation (4.1), realizing the circumstances under which its truth has certain limitations.

4.5. In practical design work it is convenient to establish what unit pressure we should allow under our foundations. Engineers designing full-size foundations normally work in units of kilonewtons per square metre (kN/m^2), as already indicated in the tables in Chapter 2. On the other hand, in certain tests and in the laboratory one sometimes still sees the use of kilograms force per square centimetre (kgf/cm^2). It is convenient to remember that $1\ kN/m^2 = 0\cdot01\ kgf/cm^2$.

The symbols normally used to denote pressures are as follows:
q = unit pressure under foundation,
q_a = safe bearing capacity of the soil,
q_f = ultimate bearing capacity of the soil.

The first step is to find the *ultimate* bearing capacity of a soil. Later we can consider what would be a *safe* bearing capacity for that soil. And then we shall talk about settlements and *allowable bearing pressures*.

Cohesive soils

4.6. When a foundation pushes down a triangular wedge of soil, as shown in Fig. 4.1, the boundary planes AB and CB get pushed away and rotate about centres very approximately at A and C, with the effect that the ground to the sides of the foundation is pushed sideways and upwards as indicated in Fig. 4.2. This matter has been studied carefully by a number of investigators, who have calculated the minimum shear resistance along the curved lines in Fig. 4.2 in relation to the unit pressure under the foundation and the weight of soil lifted at the sides. In practice the matter becomes a little complicated by the roughness of the underside of the foundation. In general terms, for foundations at ground level on plastic clays (that is, non-frictional soils, where $\phi = 0$), the ultimate bearing capacity of the soil can be expressed as

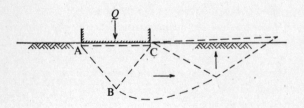

FIG. 4.2. Ultimate failure of soil under spread foundation

$$q_f = cN_c, \tag{4.6}$$

where N_c is a dimensionless coefficient.

In the case of a square pad foundation at ground level, $N_c = 6$ approximately, so that

$$q_f = 6c. \tag{4.7}$$

In other words, if we are told by the laboratory that a clay soil has a cohesive strength of $100 \, \text{kN/m}^2$ (that is $c = 100 \, \text{kN/m}^2$), then we know that the *ultimate bearing capacity* of that clay for a square pad foundation at ground level is

$$q_f = 6 \times 100 \, \text{kN/m}^2$$
$$= 600 \, \text{kN/m}^2.$$

To this it would be necessary to apply a suitable load factor to convert from *ultimate* bearing capacity to *safe* bearing capacity. This is discussed later in this chapter.

4.7. Where foundations on clays are constructed below ground level — and they usually are — the lines of shear resistance and the weight of soil lifted at the sides increase, with the result that N_c increases also. The curves shown in Fig. 4.3 are the result of a review by Skempton

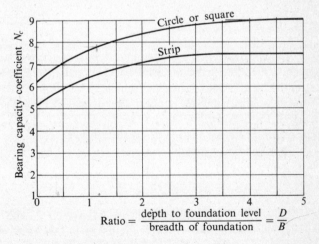

FIG. 4.3. Skempton's bearing-capacity coefficients for cohesive soils (frictionless)

of a considerable range of research work, and give N_c values for foundations with different depth/breadth ratios. The upper curve applies to the case of circular or square pads; the lower curve is for strip foundations as might be provided to support a wall. Skempton's curve shows that, where a pad foundation in clay is at a depth of 4 times the foundation breadth, N_c equals 9. This is 50 per cent greater than for a foundation sitting on clay at ground level, where N_c equals approximately 6.

For a rectangular foundation of breadth B and length L, the N_c value for the rectangle is determined from the N_c value of a square of breadth B by the equation

$$N_c \text{ (rectangle)} = \left(0\cdot84 + 0\cdot16 \frac{B}{L}\right) \times N_c \text{ (square)}. \qquad (4.8)$$

Thus, suppose for a deep foundation B = breadth = 3 m, L = length = 5 m, and D = depth = 4 m. Then, reading from the upper curve of Fig. 4.3, we see that, for a square pad foundation with $D/B = \frac{4}{3} = 1\cdot33$, N_c had the value 8·0. And for our actual rectangular foundation with $B/L = \frac{3}{5} = 0\cdot60$, we have

$$N_c = \{0\cdot84 + (0\cdot16 \times 0\cdot60)\}\, 8\cdot0$$

$$= (0\cdot84 + 0\cdot096)\, 8\cdot0$$

$$= 7\cdot5.$$

4.8. Where foundations are below ground level, a further allowance may be made to the ultimate bearing capacity of the soil for the effect of overburden. This allowance is made by adding to the value given in eqn. (4.6) an amount equal to the depth of the foundation multiplied by the effect of the bulk density of the soil. Thus if

z = the depth of the foundation below surface level,

γ = the bulk density of the soil,

eqn. (4.6) becomes

$$q_f = cN_c + \gamma z. \qquad (4.9)$$

This is a very important equation for designing foundations in clay. Consider a foundation 3 m square, at a depth of 2 m, in clay having a cohesive strength of 100 kN/m². The bulk density of the clay can be taken roughly as 2 t/m³, and this, for every metre depth of soil, will produce a pressure of 20 kN/m^2. The ratio $D/B = 2/3 = 0.66$, so from the upper curve of Fig. 4.3 we read $N_c = 7.2$. Then

$$q_f = cN_c + \gamma z$$
$$= (100 \times 7.2) + (20 \times 2) \text{ kN/m}^2$$
$$= (720 + 40) \text{ kN/m}^2$$
$$= 760 \text{ kN/m}^2.$$

The increase of 40 kN/m^2 may not look very much; but later, in §4.12, we shall see that the 720 kN/m^2 has to be reduced by a load factor of 3, whereas the 40 kN/m^2 does not.

Cohesive and frictional soils

4.9. With soils that combine cohesive and frictional qualities, the matter becomes more complicated. Nevertheless Terzaghi and Peck have found a mathematical solution for the special case of a strip footing and modified this very slightly in the light of experimental results to suit square foundations of side B, on dense or stiff soil, as follows,

$$q_f = 1.2c\,N_c + \gamma z N_q + 0.4\,\gamma B N_\gamma. \tag{4.10}$$

N_c, N_q, and N_γ are dimensionless quantities known as *bearing capacity coefficients*, and depend only on the value of ϕ. The values of these coefficients have been calculated for various ϕ values and are given in Fig. 4.4.

Thus the ultimate bearing capacity of a soil having $c = 40 \text{ kN/m}^2$ and $\phi = 15°$, for a foundation 2.5 m square at a depth of 1.5 m would be

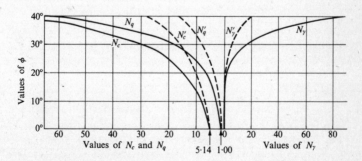

FIG. 4.4. Terzaghi and Peck's bearing-capacity coefficients for all soil types

$$q_f = (1\cdot2 \times 40 \times 12) + (20 \times 1\cdot5 \times 4) + (0\cdot4 \times 20 \times 2\cdot5 \times 2)\,\text{kN/m}^2$$
$$= (576 + 120 + 40)\,\text{kN/m}^2$$
$$= 736\,\text{kN/m}^2.$$

Eqn. (4.10) applies only for foundations on stiff or dense soils. Where soils are soft or loose, appreciable settlement of the foundation is likely to occur before general shear failure takes place. In these circumstances it is prudent to take the cohesion and friction values of the soil as only two thirds of their actual values. This is catered for by replacing eqn. (4.10) by

$$q_f = 0\cdot8cN_c' + \gamma z N_q' + 0\cdot4\gamma B N_\gamma', \qquad (4.11)$$

using the modified bearing capacity coefficients as shown dotted in Fig. 4.4.

Frictional soils

4.10. The previous sections give direct methods of calculating the ultimate bearing capacities of truly cohesive soils and soils which combine the properties of cohesion and friction. These methods rely on our first knowing the values of c and ϕ for the soils concerned; these are determined in the laboratory by tests on undisturbed samples. The undisturbed samples of both these types of soil can be taken from boreholes in the manner described later in §5.2.

However, it is impracticable to take undisturbed samples of truly frictional materials (sands and gravels) because they tend to spill, and the very act of sampling such materials causes disturbance to their natural degree of compaction. Therefore no method of calculating the strengths of cohesionless materials is given here, as in practice it is more satisfactory to rely on penetration tests carried out on such soils *in situ* in the boreholes. These are described fully in §§5.11 and 5.12.

Cartwheel failure

4.11. The form of soil failure described in §4.6 and which applies also in §4.9 is certainly the most common and would normally be met, for example, at individual column foundations for a building. However, cases have occurred where large structures supported at quite modest bearing pressures have sought out a large plane of weakness extending

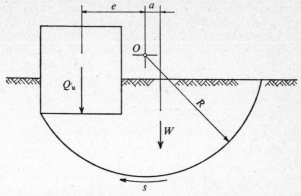

FIG. 4.5. Cartwheel failure of soil under large structure

to a considerable depth so as to produce a *cartwheel failure*, as indicated in Fig. 4.5. Here it is not the foundations of individual columns
that have failed, but the larger mass of ground supporting the building
as a whole. The instability has arisen from the weight of the structure
on one side of some centre of rotation being greater than the weight
of ground on the other side of the same centre acting in combination
with the shear resistance of the ground against rotational failure along
the arc indicated.

Analysis of this type of failure was first suggested by Fellenius. We
use the following symbols:

Q_u = the ultimate load from the structure,
 e = the eccentricity of Q about the centre of rotation,
 W = the weight of the soil mass within the arc of rotation,
 a = the eccentricity of W about the centre,
 R = the radius of the arc,
 l = the length of the arc,
 s = the shear strength of the soil.

Then, by taking moments about the centre of rotation, we have

$$Q_u e = Wa + slR,$$

whence

$$Q_u = \frac{Wa + slR}{e}. \tag{4.12}$$

The analysis is made by trying various centres of rotation until a centre is found which gives the least value for Q_u.

A check against cartwheel failure should be made in cases where the load applied to the soil is considerable and extensive and where the shear strength of the soil is known to be poor and largely non-frictional. For example, large grain-silos have been known to fail in this way.

Where the soil strength varies at different depths, the different shear strengths along the arc of rotation may be taken into account quite simply by this method.

'Ultimate' and 'safe' bearing capacities

4.12. Having now determined by the methods given in §4.6 *et seq.* what is the theoretical *ultimate* bearing capacity of the soil on which we propose to construct our foundation, we have to know what would be the *safe* bearing capacity of that soil, remembering that our laboratory tests which gave us our values of c and ϕ are likely to be in error to some extent, the samples on which these tests are made are unlikely to be truly representative of the whole of the soil at our site, and different rates of settlement of different parts of our structure may lead to parts of the foundations being loaded more heavily than we had allowed for when making our calculations.

The *safe* bearing capacity of a soil is determined by applying a suitable load factor to the *ultimate* bearing capacity. Thus if we denote the safe bearing capacity as q_a, we have

$$q_a = \frac{q_f}{F},$$

where F is the load factor. Where the expression for ultimate bearing capacity takes into account the depth the foundation is below surface level, the load factor is of course not applied to this part of the equation.

Thus for clay soils we have, from eqn. (4.9),

$$q_a = \frac{cN_c}{F} + \gamma z. \tag{4.13}$$

And for soils which combine cohesive and frictional qualities we have from eqn. (4.10)

$$q_a = \frac{(1 \cdot 2cN_c + \gamma z N_q + 0 \cdot 4\gamma BN_\gamma)}{F} + \gamma z. \tag{4.14}$$

The load factor F against ultimate shear failure is normally taken as 3. Note that with the bearing capacity of the soil being reduced in this way to give a 'safe' value, we do not increase our design load by the partial safety factor γ_f as described in §6.4; this is done only for the purpose of our concrete design work.

4.13. *Safe bearing capacity* means just exactly what it says, and nothing more. It means that foundations designed to bear on the ground at this pressure are *safe*, and the ground will not *collapse* due to the development of shear failure.

But sometimes it is not sufficient to know that the foundation is safe. In cohesive soils a perfectly safe foundation may sink or *settle* by more than an acceptable amount over a period of years. Some buildings have large sliding doors which would become jammed if the roof settled towards the floor more than a certain amount; certain buildings that are constructed with more floors at one end than the other would be quite unsatisfactory if the taller and heavier part settled more than the lower part. The reader should be able to think of other cases where excessive settlement could become an embarrassment.

The *amount* of settlement that will occur under foundation loads will of course depend on the rigidity and compressibility of the underlying strata; but the *relative* settlement of different parts of an extensive structure or building will depend also on the stiffness of the building superstructure. Settlement in sands and gravels normally occurs quickly, and often is substantially complete by the end of the construction period. This is because the pore-water referred to in §4.4 can get away easily. However, settlement in clays and silts continues slowly over periods extending several years, because of the difficulty the pore-water has in making its egress between the smaller particles.

Estimation of soil settlements is one of the most difficult aspects of foundation design; yet errors of settlement assessment can lead to as much long-term trouble as most other design considerations. One very useful way of determining the likely settlement of foundations is to go and examine the behaviour of similar structures with comparable foundations on adjacent sites; indeed the local authority engineer is likely to have records and useful advice which are worth as much as any calculation based on soil-mechanics techniques.

Nevertheless, occasions do arise where the designer is left to his own resources in this regard, and then it becomes necessary to make at least an approximate calculation based on whatever soil-survey material is available. Rough comparative methods based on the results of simple loading tests were given in §3.12. A rather more sophisticated method of assessment is given later in this chapter (§4.15 *et seq.*). Whichever methods are used, it is important to realize that accurate forecasts are virtually impossible in the present state of foundation knowledge, and the reader is warned against taking risks where large settlements could occur under important structures and buildings.

Particularly in the case of foundations built on soils that rely to any great degree on cohesion for their strength, it may often be necessary to work to lower bearing pressures than the *safe* bearing capacities. Such reduced bearing pressures would then be known as *allowable bearing pressures.*

Distribution of stress with depth

4.14. In this chapter so far we have seen how the *shear strength* of a soil is dependent on cohesion and friction. The cohesion is given directly by c, and the friction is determined from ϕ. We shall see in Chapter 5 how we obtain c and ϕ for various soils. We have seen also (§§4.6–4.12) how the *safe bearing capacity* for a soil under a foundation is determined from c and ϕ.

We are now well on our way to being able to design some real foundations. But therefore going further with this it will be well to think back to §3.11 and Fig. 3.4, where we referred to the influence a loaded foundation has on the ground at various depths below. It is one thing to know that the soil immediately beneath a foundation is strong enough, but it is also necessary to check that the ground at all layers further down is also strong enough for the duty that will be required of it. It is necessary, therefore, to understand how the applied pressure intensity under a foundation diminishes at increased depths. Then we can decide how deep to go with our exploratory boreholes and what minimum strength of soil we shall require lower down.

An approximate estimate of how the stress is distributed under a foundation can be made on the basis of simple dispersion, assuming a constant angle of, say, 30°, as shown in Fig. 4.6. The vertical applied stress p_z on a horizontal plane at depth z below a *strip* foundation is then given by

$$p_z = \frac{qB}{B + 2z \tan 30°}$$

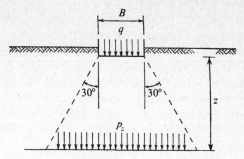

FIG. 4.6. Stress distribution by simple dispersion

or

$$p_z = q \, \frac{B}{B + 1 \cdot 5z}, \qquad (4.15)$$

where q is the applied pressure at foundation level and B is the breadth of the foundation.

A more exact method is the authors' adaptation of a graphical method first proposed by Housel (see Fig. 4.7). From the two edges of the strip foundation, lines AB, AC, and AD are drawn down to any horizon BCD where we wish to know how the stress intensities vary. Lines AB are vertical, AC slope at 2 to 1, and AD slope at 1 to 1, as indicated. The maximum applied stress at the depth z is then determined on the basis that the total applied load from the foundation be divided by the width CC. This maximum stress therefore equals

$$p_z = q \, \frac{B}{B + z}, \qquad (4.16)$$

and is assumed to extend over the width BB. Thus the points B' are marked above B to some suitable scale. Points DB' are then joined,

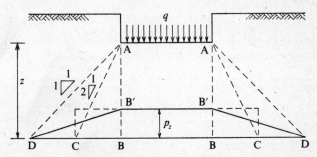

FIG. 4.7. Graphical method of determining stress dispersion

and the complete line of stress distribution is given by the line DB′B′D. This graphical method of determining applied stresses at any depths is generally sufficiently accurate for most practical purposes.

Now both the methods illustrated above at Figs 4.6 and 4.7 relate to *strip* foundations where the dispersion can occur only in two directions. With *square* foundations the dispersion occurs in four directions (that is, it spreads out from each of the four sides of the foundation), so that the stresses diminish more rapidly for a given increase of depth.

This is indicated very clearly at the graphs in Fig. 4.8, where bulbs of *constant applied vertical soil stress* have been plotted. Each bulb of constant stress has been drawn by joining up a number of points where the stress has the same value — be it $0·20q$, $0·40q$, or whatever other proportion of q may be chosen. Thus, in the same way that each contour line on a map is everywhere at some constant height above sea level so (in Fig. 4.8) each line of constant stress indicates everywhere positions where the vertical stresses in the soil are constant.

Very often in foundation design we limit the extent of our investigation of the soil to such a depth that the stresses from the foundation have diminished to about a fifth of the values immediately under the foundation itself, that is, to the level of the $0·20q$ stressbulb. In Fig. 4.8(a), for a *square* foundation, this is seen to be something less than $1\frac{1}{2}$ times the breadth of the foundation B. For a *strip* foundation, Fig. 4.8(b) shows that the same stress distribution is not

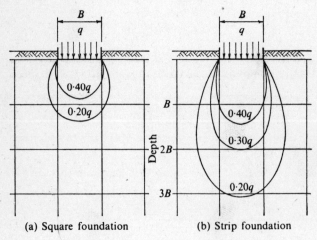

(a) Square foundation   (b) Strip foundation

FIG. 4.8. Bulbs of constant vertical soil stress

THEORY OF SOIL BEHAVIOUR 53

achieved until roughly double this depth, that is, when the depth is about 3 times the foundation breadth B.

For significant structures where the loads from the individual columns are likely to spread out so as to link up with one another and form all-embracing bulbs of stress under the structure as a whole, it is usual to carry the site investigations to a depth equal to about twice the plan dimension of the structure, and to a width of about $1\frac{1}{2}$ times. The reasons for this are clearly seen by reference to Fig. 4.8.

Consolidation settlement of clays

4.15. In §2.8 and Table 2.2 warning was given that cohesive soils are susceptible to long-term *consolidation settlement*. This is because the low permeability of these soils has the effect that, when external stresses are applied, the water contained between the small particles has great difficulty in being squeezed out and escaping. Frequently loaded clays go on consolidating over a period of years; and generally these long-term consolidation settlements are of much greater magnitude than the *immediate settlements* that occur when the foundation load is first applied. It was for this reason that it was pointed out in §4.13 that the *allowable bearing pressure* on a clay may have to be determined by considerations of settlement rather than by calculations of safety based on the shear strength of the soil.

Sands and gravels are different. Generally their movements are limited almost to the *immediate* settlement — though this can be a determining factor; furthermore they can be tested and assessed for strength only by *in situ* empirical methods, and the latter seek to contain built-in allowances for settlement effects (see §§4.10, 5.11, and 5.12). Thus sands and gravels are no part of the discussion that follows now on consolidation-settlement calculations.

4.16. One of the most important laboratory tests to be done on clay samples sent in from a site investigation is the *oedometer test*. The equipment and method of procedure is described in §5.10. It is from the results of this test that the coefficient of compressibility m_v of the soil is determined — that is, the change in unit volume per unit change in pressure — and from this coefficient we are able to calculate the amount of *consolidation settlement* likely to occur under any foundation loading.

Unfortunately an oedometer test normally takes something like a fortnight to carry out on each sample — allowing for each stage to come to rest, and for intervening weekends! — and for this reason and because of the space occupied by the equipment, oedometer tests are all too frequently skimped or omitted altogether from site-investigation studies in favour of other tests which are quicker, simpler, and cheaper to do, such as, for example, triaxial compression tests. This is clearly unwise management of a testing programme, when one realizes that many clays — certainly soft and sensitive ones — frequently have their allowable bearing capacities determined by considerations of settlement rather than of strength.

Typical values for coefficient of compressibility m_v derived from oedometer tests are given in Table 4.1. These are based on material published by Tomlinson. The consolidation settlement of a cohesive soil layer is then calculated by the formula

$$S = m_v \times p_z \times H, \tag{4.17}$$

where

S = consolidation settlement,

m_v = average coefficient of compressibility for the layer,

p_z = average applied vertical stress on the layer of depth z,

H = thickness of layer.

TABLE 4.1
Compressibility of cohesive soils

Type of soil	Compressibility	Coefficient of compressibility m_v (mm²/N)
(1) Very sensitive soft organic clays and peat	Highest	Over 1·5
(2) Alluvial clays and silts as found in meandering estuary valleys and deltas	Higher	1·5–0·3
(3) Normally consolidated clays	Medium	0·3–0·1
(4) Very stiff clays, boulder clays, keuper marl, and similar	Lower	0·1–0·05
(5) Hard clays, heavily over-consolidated boulder clays, and soft silty rocks	Lowest	0·05 and less

Types (4) and (5) are not likely to lead to settlement problems. Indeed consolidation settlements with these types are likely to be a good deal less than results calculated from oedometer readings.

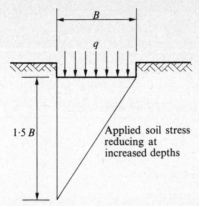

FIG. 4.9. Approximate reduction of applied soil stress under a square foundation

4.17. Eqn. (4.17) may at first appear simple enough. However, in practice the m_v values are likely to vary quite considerably about the site, and in all probability will reduce as the compressibility of the clay reduces with increasing depths. Furthermore the applied vertical stress p_z from the foundation pressure does not decrease linearly with depth, and further complications arise when the stress zones from adjacent foundations overlap. For these reasons there is difficulty too in deciding on suitable dimensions to take for the layer thickness H.

Nevertheless, bearing in mind the limitations of accuracy that apply to all soil-mechanics work, it is often reasonable to make some simplifying assumptions, particularly with clays that are not unduly soft and in cases where the loads and foundation sizes are reasonably modest. Thus Fig. 4.9 shows a simplified triangular vertical stress distribution, assumed to vary from q immediately under the foundation to zero at a depth equal to $1\frac{1}{2}$ times the foundation breadth B. The student will recognize the argument for this by referring to Fig. 4.8(a).

If then we take our layer thickness H as $1\cdot5B$, the average applied vertical stress will be $0\cdot5q$, so we can re-write eqn. (4.17) as

$$S = m_v \times 0\cdot5q \times 1\cdot5B. \tag{4.18}$$

A simple example will show how this formula can be used.

Suppose we have a column in a warehouse, carrying a load of 500 kN and needing to be founded on clay with a shear strength c of 50 kN/m², and a coefficient of compressibility m_v of $0\cdot2$ mm²/N. Will the foundation size be determined by the *safe* bearing capacity of the soil, or would this lead to unacceptable settlement requiring us to work to some reduced *allowable* bearing pressure?

To determine the bearing capacity from strength considerations let us try $N_c = 7 \cdot 0$. Then

$$q_f = 7 \cdot 0 \times 50 \, \text{kN/m}^2 = 350 \, \text{kN/m}^2,$$

and with a load factor of 3 we then have

$$q_a = \frac{350}{3} \, \text{kN/m}^2 = 117 \, \text{kN/m}^2;$$

so our foundation size will be

$$\frac{500}{117} = 4 \cdot 25 \, \text{m}^2$$

$$= 2 \cdot 10 \, \text{m} \times 2 \cdot 10 \, \text{m} \text{ (say)}.$$

If the depth D of foundation is 1 m, we then have

$$\frac{D}{B} = \frac{1 \cdot 00}{2 \cdot 10} = 0 \cdot 5 \text{ (approximately)},$$

and a check from Fig. 4.3 confirms that our choice of $7 \cdot 0$ for N_c was reasonable.

The actual pressure q under the foundation is

$$\frac{500 \, \text{kN}}{2 \cdot 10 \, \text{m} \times 2 \cdot 10 \, \text{m}} = 113 \, \text{kN/m}^2.$$

Thus using eqn. (4.18) we can calculate the consolidation settlement as

$$S = m_v \times 0 \cdot 5q \times 1 \cdot 5B$$

$$= 0 \cdot 2 \times \left(\frac{0 \cdot 5 \times 113}{10^3} \right) \times (1 \cdot 5 \times 2 \cdot 10 \times 10^3)$$

$$= 35 \, \text{mm}.$$

This amount of settlement would be acceptable for a warehouse type of building, so that the *safe* bearing pressure of 117 kN/m² is also the *allowable* bearing pressure. However, if the clay had been softer and had a higher m_v value, then the settlement at 117 kN/m² would have been correspondingly greater and unacceptable, so that some lower bearing pressure would have had to be chosen and worked to as *allowable*.

The example of settlement calculation given above was very simple. For larger foundations, and in cases where m_v is known from the laboratory tests to reduce with increasing depths, it may be realistic to consider the clay beneath the foundation as a number of horizontal layers, working out separately the settlement due to each layer, and then adding these up to arrive at the total consolidation settlement. The principle of this is indicated in Fig. 4.10. It is not likely that five equal layers would be taken each with a different m_v value as shown, but the figure represents how a varying stratum can be handled, and in particular how a check can be made on a highly compressible layer that may be known to exist at some depth below a foundation.

Another point about our example of settlement assessment given above is that the same column load was used in calculating the safe pressure q_a as for calculating the consolidation settlement. In the case of a warehouse column this would be correct; but in the case of a column which is only loaded intermittently, and in all probability

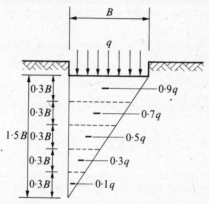

FIG. 4.10. Applied soil stress acting on a number of horizontal layers

never *fully* loaded, it is important to do the settlement calculation using a *realistic* load figure such as is likely to be sustained in the long-term. In an office building for example, q_a has to be determined on the basis that a high proportion of the floors are likely to be loaded to a considerable degree at any one time; whereas from a consolidation-settlement point of view it is the *un*likeliness of this occurring over continuous 24-hour periods that has to be borne in mind. In all probability an office building is occupied for only about a fifth of the time, and even then to something very much less than its design capacity.

Settlement craters

4.18. In significant structures where the loads from individual columns produce stress zones that spread out and overlap one another, the settlement of the total structure has to be considered as a whole. This was referred to in §4.14, where we discussed bulbs of constant vertical soil stress. The pressures from the separate columns will then even out amongst themselves, forming one large set of bulbs of stress extending down to a depth of about $1\frac{1}{2}$ times the width of the total structure. The settlement calculation will then give an indication of the *maximum settlement* at the centre of the structure; but as the deformation of the strata at this scale generally takes on the form of a *crater of depression*, the columns at the edges of the structure are likely to settle considerably less than those at the centre — often about half as much. Thus the *differential settlement* across the structure on this basis will probably be about half the value given by the use of eqns. (4.17) or (4.18).

Craters of depression are likely to occur with sandy soils just as much as with clays. The engineer has always to be on his guard. *In situ* methods for assessing suitable bearing pressures for foundations on cohesionless soils — making allowance for probable settlements — are given in §§5.11 and 5.12; these take the form of standard penetration tests and Dutch cone tests.

5

Soil-mechanics tests

5.1. In the previous chapter we showed that the bearing capacity of a soil depends on its shear strength, which in turn depends on the summation of two internal properties, namely cohesion and friction. We have seen that the relationship between the shear strength and the cohesion and friction can be expressed in a simple mathematical equation,

$$s = c + p \tan \phi.$$

If now we can measure values of c and ϕ for the particular soil on which we wish to construct a foundation, we can then determine the bearing capacity of the soil, using such formulae as were given in the previous chapter in eqns (4.6) and (4.10). The object of the present chapter is to explain how these values of c and ϕ are measured.

Standard apparatus and procedures for the various tests are described in BS 1377 (1967): *Methods of testing soils for civil engineering purposes* – and whilst the essential purposes are described in general terms in the present chapter, the student is referred to the BS 1377 for fuller details.

Undisturbed samples

5.2. Most methods used for measuring c and ϕ involve testing in a laboratory. The first thing to do, therefore, is to get *undisturbed samples* of the soil from the site to the laboratory. Normally this is done by taking the samples at convenient depths during the process of sinking the boreholes described in § 3.5. The *auger* tool is used just prior to sampling in order to reduce the amount of local disturbance in the soil.

The sampling is achieved by driving a thin-walled sampler tube (Shelby tube), of about 100 mm internal diameter, into the soil. The tube is usually well oiled inside and out to reduce friction, and then attached to the boring rods and lowered to the bottom of the borehole. It is driven into the soil either by blows from a monkey or, preferably, by jacking, which produces less disturbance. The distance through which the sampler tube is driven should be checked, as if the tube goes too far the soil will be compressed longitudinally within it. After driving, the rods and sampler are rotated to break off the core, and the sampler is steadily withdrawn.

On recovery, caps are screwed on the ends of the tube, and the sample is sent to the laboratory for examination and testing. It is important that the undisturbed samples are tested within 2 weeks of taking them from the borehole; and during this interval they are best stored in a cool room having a high humidity.

The actual *specimens* used for the laboratory tests are then carefully taken from the samples in the laboratory; these are frequently 100 mm diameter for triaxial tests (though sometimes 38 mm), 76 mm for oedometer tests, and 38 mm for unconfined compression tests.

It is impossible to overemphasize the fact that the number of un-disturbed samples taken at any site should be considerable. All real soils vary widely within themselves, even though they appear by visual inspection to be uniform; and at most sites the strata vary from depth to depth, and from position to position across the site. Thus it would be most unwise to base the design for the foundations of an important structure on the results of tests on only two or three samples taken at random depths in each of only two or three boreholes. It is unlikely that so few samples would reveal adequately the strength (and weak-nesses) of the enormous mass of soil on which we are to rely to support any extensive structure.

There are certain standard recommendations applying to the depths at which undisturbed samples should be taken, but there may well be cases for not following these recommendations too closely. If founda-tions are likely to be at, say, 1 m below ground level, this would seem to be the best level at which to be taking samples rather than intervals coming somewhat higher and then considerably lower. The maximum pressure on the ground will occur exactly at the level of the underside of the foundation, and if it is possible to assess the level at which this is likely to be, then this certainly will be the best level at which to take one's first sample in each of the boreholes.

It is, of course, impossible to obtain truly 'undisturbed' samples of any soil, because the very penetration of the sampling tube into the soil causes disturbance. With cohesive soils (clays) which are not too hard or friable, the disturbance is normally of a minor character, and the errors which arise are generally less than the variation between the soil as actually sampled and other soils elsewhere on the site which it is hoped the samples may reasonably represent.

With sands and gravels, however, the discrepancies are more pronounced, partly because the sampling tube has to push individual particles to one side in order to achieve penetration at all, and partly because the samples tend to spill out of the tube, interfering with the natural degree of compaction. For these reasons it is more reliable, and certainly simpler, to determine the strengths of sandy soils and gravels by penetration tests as described in §§ 5.11 and 5.12.

Cohesive soils

5.3. Plastic clays are the simplest soils to consider under laboratory conditions. They come very close to being truly cohesive, that is they rely for their strength almost entirely on cohesion and derive negligible benefit from internal friction forces. Thus a clay is soft and smooth to the touch. Essentially, it is not gritty.

If we take a small circular prism of clay of unit cross-sectional area (as shown in Fig. 5.1(a)) and load this miniature column as indicated, it will eventually collapse, either as shown in Fig. 5.1(b) or 5.1(c).

In Fig. 5.1(b) the two ends of our prism have sought out the weakest plane between them, and are sliding past one another at an angle of 45°. In Fig. 5.1(c) the clay is more plastic and tends to squeeze up and outwards into the shape of a barrel; then one end starts to penetrate the swollen centre of the other, until failure occurs in this manner. Either way, failure is by part of the material sliding against the other at an angle of 45°.

These diagonal planes can be seen developing while the load on the prism is being built up to its maximum value at failure, and very real

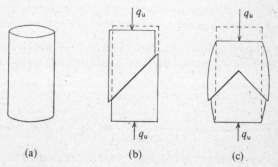

FIG. 5.1. Failure of clay prism under axial load

forces persist as between the clay on one side of the failure plane and
the clay on the other side. These forces are the cohesive strength of
the clay and, as clays have negligible internal friction strength, the
shear strength here is made up entirely by what we have agreed to call
the *cohesive strength* of the clay. Thus if

$$s = \text{the shearing resistance of the clay,}$$

$$c = \text{the cohesive strength of the clay,}$$

we can represent the relationship mathematically as

$$s = c.$$

This is the same as eqn (4.2), which we derived from Coulomb's equation.

  If the force applied on the end of our prism of unit cross-sectional
area is taken as q_u the *effectiveness* of this on a plane at $45°$ will be
less, actually $q_u/\sqrt{2}$. And the *area* of the oblique plane on which this
force acts is greater than unity, actually $\sqrt{2}$. Therefore the shear *stress*
on the plane is

$$s = \frac{\text{force}}{\text{area}} = \frac{q_u}{\sqrt{2}} \times \frac{1}{\sqrt{2}} = \frac{q_u}{2}.$$

But as $s = c$, we have

$$s = c = \frac{q_u}{2}. \tag{5.1}$$

In other words, the shear strength of the clay (which is due to its
cohesive strength) is equal to half the stress applied at the end of our
little column.

Unconfined compression test

5.4. In the laboratory it is customary to make the miniature test column
38 mm diameter and 76 mm long. This is then referred to as our
specimen.

  The specimen is held upright between two horizontal steel plates,
and squeezed axially by loading through a callibrated spring. In the
process of being squeezed longitudinally the specimen tends to swell
or bulge laterally, so in calculating the compressive stress q_u — which
of course equals load divided by area — this lateral swelling has to be
taken into the reckoning.

This very simple test is still used in parts of America, though in Britain it has normally been replaced by the triaxial compression test described in § 5.8, which is a more general case of the same thing. However, on sites where the soil is found to be consistently non-frictional and of a softish nature, and where many tests are required, the *unconfined compression test* is still of use and very convenient by virtue of the fact that the equipment required is both simple and readily portable.

5.5. It is instructive to follow through the use of our result from the unconfined compression test as follows.

The ultimate bearing capacity of a cohesive soil under a square pad foundation at ground level was given at eqn (4.7) as approximately

$$q_f = 6c.$$

But we have just shown in eqn (5.1) that

$$s = c = \frac{q_u}{2}.$$

Therefore

$$q_f = 6 \times \frac{q_u}{2} = 3q_u.$$

But in § 4.12 we showed that the safe bearing capacity of a soil q_a is given by

$$q_a = \frac{q_f}{F} = \frac{q_f}{3}.$$

Therefore

$$q_a = \frac{3q_u}{3} = q_u. \tag{5.2}$$

Thus if, for example, the unconfined compression strength of our soil had been, say, 75 kN/m^2, then we should have known that the *safe bearing capacity* of the soil would have been 75 kN/m^2 too.

Shear-vane test

5.6. It occasionally happens that a clay is so soft and sensitive that it is likely to undergo considerable change when disturbed. For such clays

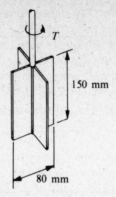

FIG. 5.2. Attachment for shear-vane test

the unconfined compression test is not entirely suitable, and the shear strength of the clay is determined *in situ* in the borehole. This is done by forcing the cruciform vane, shown in Fig. 5.2, into the clay about 0·6 m below the bottom of the borehole casing, and twisting the control rod at a specified rate and measuring the torque T.

This shear-vane test is relatively fussy and expensive to carry out, and the results obtained can be erratic and unreliable. Normally it can be applied only to clays that are so soft and sensitive one would be seeking a foundation solution that did not rely on them anyway! Accordingly the test is not much used, but nevertheless is one the student should have heard about.

Shear-box test

5.7. Before describing the most commonly used laboratory test, known as the triaxial compression test (see § 5.8), it is convenient to refer to the *shear-box test*, because this latter demonstrates well the principle of graphical representation of Coulomb's equation. In practice, the shear-box test is seldom used nowadays, except for testing coarse sands and gravels in rather particular circumstances.

The apparatus for the shear-box test is shown in Fig. 5.3(a). Essentially, it consists of a box split in two parts about a horizontal centre. The soil specimen is packed into the box, and one part of the box is then moved horizontally in relation to the other while different normal loads are applied across the plane of rupture as indicated. Records are made of the horizontal shearing force required to produce rupture for the different normal loads applied in each case.

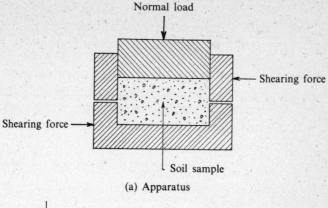

(a) Apparatus

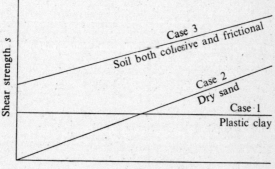

(b) Graph of results

FIG. 5.3. Shear-box test

Three typical test results are indicated at Fig. 5.3(b), where the shearing strength is plotted against the normal pressure. Case 1 is for a plastic clay, which is entirely cohesive, and therefore the shear strength is constant and quite independent of the normal stress applied. Case 2 is for a dry sand, which, being truly frictional, has a shear strength directly proportional to the normal stress, and therefore equal to zero when the normal stress is zero. Case 3 is for a soil which combines cohesive and frictional properties.

Each of the soils indicated at Fig. 5.3(b) represents graphically Coulomb's equation

$$s = c + p \tan \phi,$$

as the student should now be able to demonstrate for himself. (The tests described above are *quick undrained tests*, so we need not worry here about pore-water pressure referred to at § 4.4.)

Triaxial compression test

5.8. The *triaxial compression test* is used for testing soils which combine cohesive and frictional properties. The apparatus used is indicated at Fig. 5.4. This is probably the most normally used routine test in soils laboratories today.

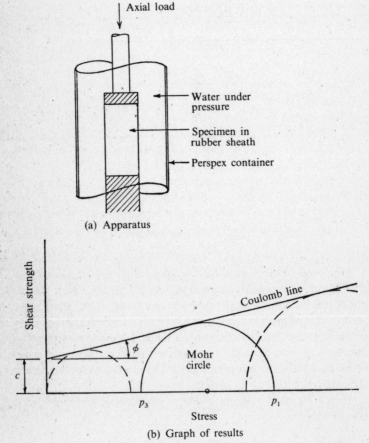

(a) Apparatus

(b) Graph of results

FIG. 5.4. Triaxial compression test

Sometimes the cylindrical specimen is the same size as used for the unconfined compression test, that is 38 mm in diameter and 76 mm long, though recently it has become more common to use larger samples up to about 100 mm diameter and 200 mm long.

The specimen is contained in a rubber sheath and surrounded by water housed in a perspex container. A hydraulic pump is used to build up the pressure of the water to any value required, and the vertical load is then applied to the end of the specimen until failure occurs.

Let p_1 be the total vertical pressure, and p_3 the lateral pressure. Then for any test the result is plotted as shown at Fig. 5.4(b), p_1 and p_3 being marked off along the base of the graph, and a Mohr semi-circle constructed above the base, passing through p_1 and p_3. A number of tests are made in this way, and a number of Mohr semicircles drawn as indicated. A line is then drawn just touching the tops of the semicircles (the tangent to the semicircles), and it can be demonstrated that this line represents Coulomb's equation in the same way as the lines we saw in Fig. 5.3(b).

This is a most convenient result, and can be used for testing all soils which have sufficient cohesion to enable undisturbed samples to be taken and brought to the laboratory. Indeed, with the triaxial compression-test apparatus one can determine values of c and ϕ for most soils other than sands and gravels.

Note that the unconfined compression test described in § 5.4 is merely a special case of the triaxial compression test, but suitable only for cohesive soils where the frictional contribution is negligible.

5.9. Our results from the triaxial compression test are made use of as follows.

For a frictionless soil we apply our value of c in eqn (4.6). For other soils we apply our values for c and ϕ in eqn (4.10). In either case the result we obtain is the ultimate bearing capacity of the soil, to which it is necessary to apply a suitable load factor to convert to the safe bearing capacity as described in § 4.12.

In cases where cartwheel failure needs to be considered, we apply our values for c and ϕ in Coulomb's equation so as to determine s (the shear strength of the soil); and then we carry out the analysis proposed by Fellenius using eqn (4.12).

Oedometer test

5.10. We have made much reference to *settlement* as a determining factor in foundation design, irrespective of whatever may be *safe*. It is no use having a building which is safe, but nevertheless so distorted by settlement that the doors and windows jam, and the plaster and other

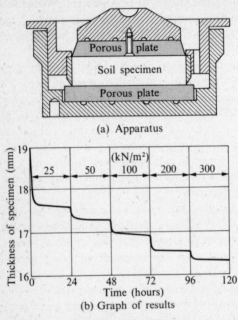

(a) Apparatus

(b) Graph of results

FIG. 5.5. Oedometer test

finishes crack and are disfigured. In §§ 4.16 and 4.17 we showed how consolidation settlement can be calculated from the results of oedometer tests; the equipment and method of procedure for this test is now described.

The basic form of the oedometer is shown in Fig. 5.5(a). The soil specimen — normally 76 mm diameter and about 19 mm thick — is contained within a flat cylindrical ring between two circular porous stones fed with water from a reservoir. A load is applied to the upper stone, and the compression of the specimen measured on a dial gauge at predetermined intervals of time until no further compression takes place, usually after 24 hours. The load is then increased step by step and the test repeated for each increment. Typical results of such a test are illustrated in Fig. 5.5(b).

After the final load has been applied and the maximum settlement measured, the specimen is unloaded step by step allowing full recovery at each stage, the recovery being measured as before. When the specimen is fully unloaded its final height is measured.

From the results of this test we are able to determine m_v, the coefficient of compressibility of the soil, and thus the actual settlement of a full-sized foundation system as described in § 4.17.

Standard penetration test

5.11. For sands and gravels it is impracticable to obtain undisturbed samples, because of spillage and rearrangement of the particles. Nevertheless the bearing capacity of the soil can be determined by empirical penetration tests. In Britain and America the penetration of the tool is normally achieved by *dynamic* means: in Holland and some other parts of Europe the penetration is by means of a *static* pressure — see § 5.12.

The *standard penetration test* originates from America, and is made in boreholes at various levels as the boreholes are being sunk. After all debris from the boring operation has been removed, a standard sampling tube of 50 mm diameter attached to the end of a rod is driven into the soil, using a 310 kg hammer dropping 760 mm for every blow. The number of blows required to drive the tool a distance of 300 mm into the soil is counted, and known as the *penetration value N* of the soil at the depth of the test.

Terzaghi has related N to the *allowable* bearing capacities of dry or moist sands for footings of different breadths B, on the basis that the maximum settlement of the foundation should not exceed 25 mm, or the differential settlement 18 mm. This relationship is indicated in Fig. 5.6. For saturated sands the allowable bearing pressure should be reduced by 50 per cent for foundations near the surface, and by 33 per cent for foundations constructed at a depth below the surface equal to the foundation breadth B.

As an example of the use of the standard penetration test, suppose we had to carry a load of 3000 kN on a dry sand where the penetration value N was 30 blows. We see from Fig. 5.6 that a foundation 3 m wide would be suitable for an allowable pressure of about 330 kN/m², so that a foundation 3 m square would carry a load of

$$3 \text{ m} \times 3 \text{ m} \times 330 \text{ kN/m}^2 = 3000 \text{ kN}.$$

This would be satisfactory.

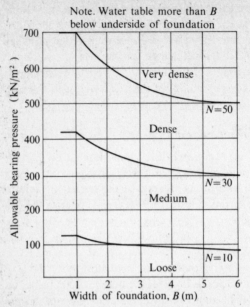

FIG. 5.6. Terzaghi's relationship between standard penetration test values and allowable bearing capacities for footings on sands

Standard penetration tests are very useful for making assessments in sands and gravels, but it has to be appreciated that the results are only *comparative*. Therefore unless there is some previous experience of a similar material it may be wise to do a simple loading test as described in § 3.8 and compare the results of this with the penetration values in a borehole immediately alongside in order to get some check on the meaningfulness of the N values; this is particularly so in cases of low N values. It has to be realized that one is much in the hands of the rig operator here, and the authors have had experience of different operators working through the same materials and getting rather different results from one another.

Other points worth watching for are as follows. If the sub-soil consists of gravel containing large pieces of boulder size, the number of blows on the tool can be deceptively high. Great care also is needed when working in waterlogged conditions, since upward water movements may disturb the very sand grains that are being tested; and under these circumstances it is important to ensure that the borehole is kept permanently flooded.

For large rafts or deep piers on dry sands, the allowable bearing pressures given in Fig. 5.6 can be increased quite considerably to arrive at results giving the same amounts of settlement; but foundation design of this nature is outside the scope of this book.

Dutch cone test

5.12. The *Dutch cone penetration test* originates from Holland, where the Dutch engineers had special problems in assessing the allowable bearing capacities of the relatively loose, sandy soils in maritime works in their low-lying terrain. The test is now much used in Belgium, Scandinavia, and elsewhere. The merit of the test is that no borehole is required, so that the tested soil really is undisturbed. The problem, however, is to understand how to convert the results of the tests, when these are carried out in territories where there is not the same background of experience as exists in Holland.

Basically the apparatus comprises a 60° cone with a diameter of about 36 mm, giving an end-area of 10 cm^2. The cone is attached to a rod — protected by passing loosely in a sleeve — and is pushed into the ground at a standard rate, the *pressure* C_d on the end of the cone being measured in kgf/cm^2 on a gauge connected to a hydraulic cylinder. Readings can be taken continuously as the cone is forced through the soil — the friction on the rod being eliminated throughout by virtue of the sleeve, which is driven to follow the rod step-by-step. The test is simple and quick to perform.

To convert the results of the Dutch cone test to an allowable bearing pressure for use in foundation design, it is often assumed the cone end-pressure (kgf/cm^2) can be divided by a factor, frequently taken as 4, to arrive at the penetration value N, allowing use to be made of Terzaghi's relationship shown in Fig. 5.6. However, there is evidence to suggest a realistic factor can vary with medium and coarser sands up to as much as 10, and with gravels — which are really inappropriate for this test — to higher than even this. Nevertheless on the simple basis that the N value is a quarter the static cone pressure C_d (kgf/cm^2), an approximate value for the allowable bearing pressure for the foundation design is then roughly

$$q_a = \frac{C_d}{0\cdot 4} \text{ kN/m}^2. \tag{5.3}$$

Classification tests

5.13. It would not be out of place here to refer briefly to *classification tests*. These do not give us specific data for enabling the bearing capacity of a given soil to be determined, but they do indicate the *condition* of a soil as it has been found *in situ*.

Thus, cohesionless soils (sandy soils) are often described as being found in a 'dense', 'medium', or 'loose' condition. The vagueness of these descriptions can be eliminated as follows.

The *voids ratio* of a soil is defined by the ratio

$$\frac{\text{volume of voids}}{\text{volume of soil particles}}$$

and, if

e = the voids ratio of the soil in its natural state,

e_0 = the voids ratio of the soil when rearranged into its loosest state,

e_{min} = the voids ratio of the soil when rearranged into its densest state,

then the *relative density* of the soil as found is given by the formula

$$\gamma_r = \frac{e_0 - e}{e_0 - e_{min}}. \tag{5.4}$$

When γ_r is less than $\frac{1}{3}$, the soil is said to be 'loose'; when γ_r is between $\frac{1}{3}$ and $\frac{2}{3}$, the soil is regarded as 'medium'; and when γ_r is greater than $\frac{2}{3}$ the soil is known as 'dense'.

Similarly, cohesive soils (clayey soils) are described according to their plasticity — the ease with which they may be moulded to shape by manipulation in the hand—the plasticity depending upon the water content of the soil. Thus we have the *liquid limit*, which is the minimum moisture content at which the soil will flow under its own weight; the addition of further water would change the soil from its plastic state into a liquid. And at the other extreme we have the *plastic limit*, which is the minimum moisture content at which the soil can be rolled into a thread 3 mm diameter without breaking; any less water would change the soil from its plastic state into a solid. These are known as the *consistency limits*.

Now, if

w = the water content of the soil as found,

w_p = the water content at the plastic limit,

w_1 = the water content at the liquid limit,

then the *liquidity index* of the soil as found is given by the expression

$$\gamma = \frac{w - w_p}{w_1 - w_p}. \tag{5.5}$$

When γ approaches unity, the soil is very soft to the extent of being pretty well liquid; and when γ approaches zero, the soil is verging on the hard solid state.

6

Spread foundations

6.1. This chapter seeks to show how spread foundations of different types may be designed; and a number of worked examples are included. But first it is appropriate to consider what different types of spread foundations are available, and why one type is used in preference to another.

The simplest form of spread foundation is a continuous *strip foundation* for supporting a wall. This type of foundation is used for domestic dwellings, and for larger buildings where load-bearing walls are employed.

For framed buildings, where the superstructure loads reach the foundations through separate columns, the simplest foundation is provided by an *independent pad* or *base* under each column.

Sometimes the adjacent columns in each row come relatively close to one another, in which case it is a convenience to link the bases between columns so as to form column strip foundations. This may facilitate excavation work, particularly when the foundations have to be fairly deep. Where columns and walls occur together at the same structure, column strip foundations serve to carry both the columns and the walls.

Where column loads are considerable, or the bearing capacity of the soil is poor, independent column bases may become so large as nearly to touch one another. It then becomes economical to link up the bases to form one continuous slab or *raft,* because the stiffer bending characteristics of a continuous slab of this form make for economy in the reinforced-concrete work. Further economies arise with raft construction because the excavation work is simpler, and the amount of edge-shuttering is considerably reduced. Often the bending and fixing of steel reinforcement is also simplified. Where the areas of independent column foundations exceed half the total area of the building, it normally becomes economical to provide a raft foundation. Where continuous retaining walls are required at the sides of a building basement, and where external asphalt protection or other waterproof membrane is involved, there are further advantages in using a raft.

Where the bearing capacity of the soil is so poor that even a normal raft could not distribute the load sufficiently, there may be a solution in constructing a *buoyant foundation*. In essence this is a deep, hollow raft, itself lighter than the weight of soil removed in the excavation. Thus the ground under the foundation experiences a relief by the removal of the soil, and this relief is available on the credit side of the soil's bearing-capacity account, and stands available for meeting the demands of supporting the loads from the superstructure. This was described in greater detail in § 1.7.

6.2. In designing spread foundations it is necessary to ensure that the undersides of the foundations are not too near the ground surface. This is because soils swell and heave or shrink and settle depending on the changes in the temperature and moisture content of the ground.

Clays swell when wetted, and shrink again on drying. These effects die out deeper down where the clay reaches a stable condition, beyond the influence of seasonal variations. Foundations in clay constructed 1 m below ground level are generally satisfactory.

Fine sands, silts, and chalk suffer from what is known as *frost heave*. This is the lifting of the ground due to the expansion of water in the soil when it freezes to form ice. Normally, foundations constructed 0·6 m below ground level are deep enough to escape the effects of frost but in regions where the frost is known to go further down than this, it is sound practice to have the underside of the foundation below the deepest level to which the frost penetrates.

6.3 Certain soils disintegrate or spoil on exposure to the air. In particular, shales crumble; clays shrink and crack in dry weather; and clays and chalk soften in wet weather, particularly if puddled by men walking on them. Sands and gravels tend to work loose if disturbed by machinery or men walking.

It is good practice, as soon as the excavation for a foundation has been completed, to put down a layer of weak plain concrete, known as blinding, 50 mm or 75 mm thick, to protect the formation.

Reinforced-concrete design

6.4. The design calculations which occupy the remainder of this book assume a knowledge of the main principles of reinforced-concrete design. They are based on the limit-state method and in this respect follow the procedure set out in CP 110: *The structural use of concrete* (1972).

It is impossible to arrive by calculation at any precise margin there may be between the *failure* strength of the reinforced concrete in a foundation and the load to which that foundation is likely to be subjected at any time in its life. This is due partly to the uncertainty of the maximum *loads* that will actually be applied to the foundation, and partly to the variations in the *strength* properties of the concrete and steel of which the foundation is comprised. Acknowledging this, the limit-state method of design sets out to achieve an acceptable level of risk so that the foundation will not become unfit for use during the life of the building or, in the terms of CP 110, that it will not reach a *limit state*.

So far as risk of overload on the reinforced concrete is concerned, a *partial safety factor* γ_f is always applied to the *characteristic load* F_k so that

$$\text{design load} = \gamma_f F_k. \tag{6.1}$$

Different partial safety factors apply in different circumstances, but in this book we shall restrict ourselves to characteristic *dead* loads G_k and characteristic *imposed* loads Q_k, which can be regarded as producing design loads of

and
$$1\cdot4\,G_k \text{ (for dead load)}$$
$$1\cdot6\,G_k \text{ (for imposed load)},$$

where $1\cdot4$ and $1\cdot6$ are the appropriate values for the partial safety factors. In the cases we shall be considering, the dead load will generally be equal to or greater than the imposed load, so for convenience we shall always be taking a compromise value of $1\cdot5$ for our partial safety factor on loads when designing our reinforced concrete work.

So far as materials are concerned, the *characteristic strengths* are taken as slightly below the ultimate values. (Normally for concrete the characteristic strength is the value below which not more than 5 per cent of the cube test results fall. The characteristic strength for reinforcement is arrived at similarly, but related to the yield or proof strength of the steel.) The reinforced-concrete work is then designed to strengths which are reduced by dividing the *characteristic strengths* f_k of each of the materials by the appropriate *partial safety factors* γ_m, so that

$$\text{design strength} = \frac{f_k}{\gamma_m}. \tag{6.2}$$

This then takes account of the risk that the materials in the actual foundation on site may be poorer than the samples tested away at the laboratory. The design examples in this book use simplified formulae, and an appropriate design chart, based on the characteristic strengths of the materials and the partial safety factors referred to in this section.

6.5. There are a number of symbols used in the reinforced concrete examples which are generally as follows:

A_s = area of tension reinforcement (mm^2),
b = width of section (mm),
d = effective depth of tension reinforcement (mm),
f_{cu} = characteristic concrete cube strength (N/mm^2),
f_y = characteristic strength of reinforcement (N/mm^2),
M = bending moment due to ultimate loads (kN m),
M_u = ultimate moment of resistance (kN m),
Q = load (kN),
V = shear force due to ultimate loads (kN),
v = shear stress in concrete (N/mm^2),
z = lever arm (mm).

The concrete used will be Grade 25, having a characteristic cube strength of 25 N/mm^2 and a design shear strength under ultimate loads, for the percentages of tension reinforcement which will be used, of 0·35 N/mm^2. The reinforcement will be high-yield steel having a characteristic strength of 425 N/mm^2.

For reinforced-concrete design the following formulae will frequently be needed.

The area of tensile reinforcement required in a member subject to bending is given by

$$A_s = \frac{M}{\left(\frac{1}{\gamma_m} \cdot f_y\right)z} = \frac{M}{(0\cdot87 f_y) \times (0\cdot9\, d)}. \tag{6.3}$$

A check on the concrete cube strength is made by the relationship

$$\frac{M_u}{bd^2} = 0\cdot15 f_{cu}. \tag{6.4}$$

The shear stress value of $0.35\,\text{N/mm}^2$ must not be exceeded on the basis that

$$v = \frac{V}{bd}. \tag{6.5}$$

A knowledge of these formulae is sufficient to follow the examples in this book but if a more thorough understanding of the design of reinforced concrete is required, the student should refer to the companion volume *Reinforced concrete simply explained* by John Faber and David Alsop.

6.6. It should also be noted that the allowable ground-bearing capacities taken in the following examples would in practice be determined by methods given earlier in this book, using either the soil-mechanics tests described in Chapter 5 or the results of a test load as described in Chapter 3. Alternatively, for approximate or preliminary calculations, the tables of safe bearing capacities given in Chapter 2 may be used.

At various stages in the calculations which follow, the figures are rounded-off in an easy way. There is no purpose in seeking to achieve greater arithmetical accuracy when we know perfectly well that our knowledge of the strengths of the soil and the concrete is far from being exact. Indeed the reader should be wary of working to a number of significant figures which are beyond the sense of the information on which the calculations are based.

Wall strip foundation

6.7. The simplest form of spread foundation to design is a continuous strip to support a wall. This has bending in only one direction.

Very frequently wall foundations are still proportioned uneconomically by out-dated rule-of-thumb methods. The provision of stepped footings, that is, widening the brickwork at the bottom, which was traditionally used with load-bearing brick walls is, of course, quite unnecessary with reinforced-concrete foundations. A single example will demonstrate this.

The wall shown in Fig. 6.1 carries a characteristic load of $120\,\text{kN}$ for every metre run. For such a purpose it is probable the ground bearing capacity would be determined from trial pits by visual inspection or simple tests as described in Chapter 3. If we found we were on a clay site, Table 3.1 would guide us towards a general description of the clay which, for example, might be a *firm* clay,

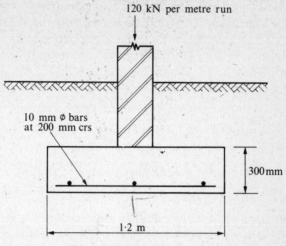

FIG. 6.1. Wall strip foundation

in which case reference to Table 2.2 would indicate the safe bearing
capacity would be of the order of $100\,kN/mm^2$. For a two-storey
building on a site where the ground is reasonably uniform, the
allowable bearing pressure would be taken as the same as the *safe*
bearing pressure, so we should design our foundation on the figure of
$100\,kN/m^2$. The width of the strip is therefore

$$\frac{120\,kN/m}{100\,kN/m^2} = 1\cdot2\,m.$$

The maximum bending moment per metre run in a case like this is
approximately

$$M = \frac{QL}{8} \tag{6.6}$$

and, remembering that for our reinforced-concrete design work we
have to increase the characteristic load of $120\,kN$ by our partial safety
factor of $1\cdot5$, we have for every metre run

$$M = \frac{(120 \times 1\cdot5)\,kN \times 1\cdot2\,m}{8}$$

$$= 27\,kN\,m.$$

If we make the foundation 300 mm thick, the effective depth of the tension reinforcement will be 300 mm less the thickness of concrete cover required outside the bars to give the necessary protection and less half the diameter of the bars themselves. Allowing 40 mm for the concrete cover, d in our case will be approximately 255 mm. Then from eqn (6.3), for every metre run

$$A_s = \frac{M}{(0.87 \, f_y) \times (0.9 \, d)}$$

$$= \frac{27 \times (10^3 \, N) \times (10^3 \, mm)}{(0.87 \times 425 \, N/mm^2) \times (0.9 \times 255 \, mm)}$$

$$= 318 \, mm^2.$$

An alternative method of arriving at the area of steel required is by use of the Design Chart shown on page 100, prepared for 425 N/mm² steel. First we calculate

$$\frac{M}{bd^2} = \frac{27 \times (10^3 \, N) \times (10^3 \, mm)}{(1000 \, mm) \times (255 \, mm)^2}$$

$$= 0.42 \, N/mm^2.$$

Then from the Design Chart

$$\frac{100 \, A_s}{bd} = 0.11,$$

giving

$$A_s = \frac{0.11 \times (1000 \, mm) \times (255 \, mm)}{100}$$

$$= 281 \, mm^2.$$

The small discrepancy between 318 mm² and 281 mm² is partly due to inaccuracies in reading the chart and partly to the effect, in eqn (6.3), of taking the approximate value of $0.9d$ for the lever arm. Such a discrepancy is of no significance bearing in mind the greater uncertainties of the bearing capacity of the soil and the variability of the strengths of the concrete and the steel.

To satisfy the requirements of the Code of Practice, we must ensure that the reinforcing steel provided is not less than 0.15 per cent of bd, where b is the breadth of the section and d is the effective depth. In our case, this gives an area of $(0.15 \times 1000\,\text{mm} \times 255\,\text{mm})/100 = 383\,\text{mm}^2$, which is greater than the area of $318\,\text{mm}^2$ required to resist the bending moment due to ultimate loads.

We must, therefore, provide not less than $383\,\text{mm}^2$ of reinforcement and this can conveniently be done using 10 mm diameter bars arranged at 200 mm centres (area $= 393\,\text{mm}^2$). In addition, three 10 mm bars are arranged longitudinally, and wired to the crossbars, and this makes for a rigid mesh which helps keep the bars properly in position while the concrete is being placed and compacted.

Independent base, loaded concentrically

6.8. Let us now design the foundation for an independent column such as we might get at the bottom of a framed building. This could be part of a block of offices or flats, for example. The column is 350 mm × 350 mm in cross-section and carries a characteristic load of 1200 kN.

In such a case, the safe and allowable bearing capacities of the soil would normally be determined from tests on undisturbed samples taken from a borehole survey, and use of appropriate formulae from Chapter 4. Let us suppose our site is composed of good firm soil, and laboratory tests on our samples give values of $c = 22\,\text{kN/m}^2$, $\phi = 20°$, and $\gamma = 18\,\text{kN/m}^2$: then eqn (4.14) will be suitable for our purpose. With *concentrically* loaded foundations near ground level, we normally work to *net* pressures, that is pressures which ignore the term γz in eqn (4.14): then we can ignore also the self-weight of the foundation, neglecting the difference in weight between the concrete foundation and the soil it replaces. Thus we have from eqn (4.14) the safe bearing capacity as

$$q_a = \frac{(1.2cN_c + \gamma z N_q + 0.4\gamma B N_\gamma)}{F},$$

where, from Fig. 4.4, we have

$$N_c = 15, N_q = 7, \text{ and } N_\gamma = 3.$$

If we assume that the depth z to the underside of the foundation is 1.5 m, and we adopt a value of 3 for the load factor F, we get, by substituting in the formula,

$$q_a = \frac{(1.2 \times 22 \times 15) + (18 \times 1.5 \times 7) + (0.4 \times 18 \times 2.45 \times 3)}{3}$$

$$= 213\,\text{kN/m}^2,$$

which we can round off to $200\,\text{kN/m}^2$ *net*.

A check then needs to be made on the settlement characteristics of
the soil, all as described in § 4.13, and if these do not predict any
unacceptable displacements, the figure of $200 \, kN/m^2$ can be taken
also as the <u>allowable bearing pressure</u> for the foundation.

The area of foundation required is therefore

$$\frac{1200 \, kN}{200 \, kN/m^2} = 6 \, m^2,$$

which is given by a foundation 2·45 m × 2·45 m. A suitable thickness
would be 500 mm (see Fig. 6.2).

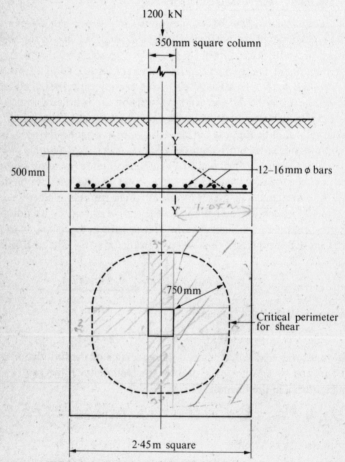

FIG. 6.2. Independent base, concentrically loaded

In a case like this, where the foundation is bending in two directions at right angles, the maximum bending moment across the foundation in any direction may be taken as approximately

$$M = \frac{QL}{12}.$$

a.v. factor $\frac{1}{2}(1\cdot9+1\cdot6)$ (6.7)

Then, in our case, the design load is $(1200 \times 1\cdot5)$ kN and

$$M = \frac{(1200 \times 1\cdot5)\,\text{kN} \times 2\cdot45\,\text{m}}{12}$$

$$= 367\,\text{kN m.}$$

This requires an area of reinforcing steel

$$A_s = \frac{M}{(0\cdot87 f_y) \times (0\cdot9 d)}$$

$$= \frac{(367 \times 10^6)}{(0\cdot87 \times 425) \times (0\cdot9 \times 435)}\,\text{mm}^2$$

$$= 2535\,\text{mm}^2.$$

As in § 6.7, a slightly more accurate assessment of the reinforcing steel required, which does not depend upon estimating the value of the lever arm z, can be made by using the Design Chart:

$$\frac{M}{bd^2} = \frac{(367 \times 10^6)}{2450 \times 435^2}\,\text{N/mm}^2$$

$$= 0\cdot79\,\text{N/mm}^2;$$

hence

$$\frac{100 A_s}{bd} = 0\cdot22$$

and

$$A_s = \frac{0\cdot22 \times 2450 \times 435}{100}\,\text{mm}^2$$

$$= 2345\,\text{mm}^2.$$

This is provided by twelve 16 mm diameter bars (area = 2410 mm²). The same amount of bending occurs in both directions at right-angles, so it is necessary to provide the reinforcements both ways in the base.

To ensure that the compressive stress in the concrete does not exceed the characteristic strength of 25 N/mm² for our mix we must check that, in accordance with eqn (6.4),

$$\frac{M}{bd^2} \text{ does not exceed } 0.15 \times 25 \text{ N/mm}^2 = 3.75 \text{ N/mm}^2.$$

We have already found that in our case $M/bd^2 = 0.79$ N/mm², which is less than 3.75 N/mm², and the concrete stress is therefore satisfactory.

It now remains only to check the shear strength of the foundation. Shear failure in a case like this generally occurs by the column punching a more or less pyramid-shaped piece of concrete out of the bottom of the foundation, as shown dotted in the section and plan of Fig. 6.2.

The critical section for shear is 1.5 D from the face of the column where D is the over-all depth of the foundation, which in our case is 1.5 × 500 mm = 750 mm, giving a total perimeter at the critical shear section of

$$(4 \times 350 \text{ mm}) + (2 \times \pi \times 750 \text{ mm}) = 6110 \text{ mm}.$$

The base of our pyramid, of course, bears directly on the ground at the safe bearing pressure of 200 kN/m² so that this part of our total load of 1200 kN presents no shear across the critical section.

The area within the perimeter of the critical section is

$$\frac{350 \text{ mm}^2 + (4 \times 350 \text{ mm} \times 750 \text{ mm}) + (\pi \times 750^2 \text{ mm}^2)}{10^6}$$

$$= 2.94 \text{ m}^2,$$

compared with a total area for the base of 6 m².

The load outside the area of the base of the pyramid which produces shear on our critical perimeter of 6110 mm is

$$\frac{1200 \text{ kN} \times (6 - 2.94) \text{ m}^2}{6 \text{ m}^2}$$

$$= 612 \text{ kN}.$$

This figure is based on the characteristic load of 1200 kN, and before checking the shear stress against the ultimate value for the section it must be multiplied by our partial safety factor of 1.5. Hence the design shear force V is 612 × 1.5 kN = 918 kN.

Now, the shear stress v is given by the formula

$$v = \frac{V}{pd}, \tag{6.8}$$

where p is the perimeter of the critical section and d is the effective depth. So that in our case we have

$$v = \frac{(918 \times 10^3)}{6100 \times 435} \, \text{N/mm}^2$$

$$= 0.34 \, \text{N/mm}^2,$$

which — as it is less than $0.35 \, \text{N/mm}^2$, the value of the permissible shear stress given in § 6.5 — is satisfactory.

If either the compressive stress in the concrete or the shear stress had been greater than the permissible values, the simplest method of overcoming the problem would have been to increase the thickness of the base and repeat the design procedure including the checks on the concrete stresses.

6.9. A more exact method of calculating the bending moment in the previous example would be as follows.

The critical section for bending is assumed to be at the face of the column, that is, at YY in Fig. 6.2. The upward force to the right of YY due to ultimate loads is

$$= 2.45 \, \text{m} \times 1.05 \, \text{m} \times 200 \, \text{kN/m}^2 \times 1.5$$

$$= 773 \, \text{kN},$$

so that the bending moment at YY is

$$M = 773 \times \frac{1.05}{2}$$

$$= 405 \, \text{kN m}.$$

This compares with the 367 kN m obtained by the simple formula (6.7). The reason for showing here the more exact method of calculation is that, when we come to eccentrically loaded bases, there is no alternative simple approach, and the fuller calculation becomes necessary.

The sections which follow (§§ 6.10 and 6.11) may be omitted on first reading if the reader finds the calculations difficult to follow.

Independent base, loaded eccentrically, within middle third

6.10. In the previous example we designed a foundation for a column carrying a direct central load, where the load from the column was applied centrally on the foundation and centrally on the ground. Frequently in practice this happy state of affairs does not occur. For example, if the column is carrying a long, slender beam, the beam will deflect, and in this way will bend the top of the column; and depending on whether the column carries on above the level of the beam and how stiff the column is, part of the bending induced in the column will be transferred down to the foundation. Bending at the feet of columns arises also from horizontal sway effects, such as from wind forces and overhead crane surge.

Where foundations have to perform the duty of resisting both a direct load and an applied bending moment together we can consider the effect as being the same as if a direct load of equal magnitude were applied at some definite *eccentricity*. Thus the foundation would be *eccentrically loaded*. Suppose the total load is Q and the bending moment is M, then the eccentricity is given by

$$e = \frac{M}{Q}. \qquad (6.9)$$

In considering the centrally loaded foundation in § 6.8 we ignored the self-weight of the foundation, and worked to the *net* bearing capacity of the soil at ground level. However, with foundations which are required to cater for out-of-balance bending effects, the weight of the foundation is normally included in the calculation because it assists in providing the necessary stabilizing balance. Then we have to work to the *gross* bearing capacity of the soil.

Let us take a definite example. A column 250 mm × 250 mm carries a direct load of 400 kN and a bending moment of 150 kN m. It is required to design a suitable foundation to support this column on ground which has a safe *gross* bearing capacity of 250 kN/m^2.

A rectangular base will give stability against bending better than a square base. We will try a base 2·65 m × 1·2 m × 500 mm thick as shown in Fig. 6.3. Then

column load	400 kN
weight of base	36 kN
total load Q	436 kN.

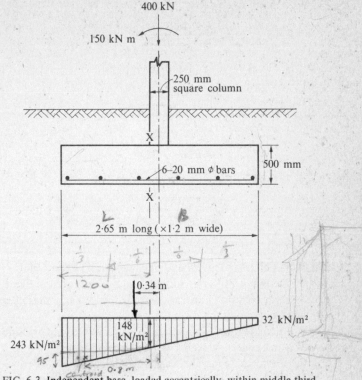

FIG. 6.3. Independent base, loaded eccentrically, within middle third

Therefore the eccentricity is

$$e = \frac{M}{Q} = \frac{150\,\text{kN m}}{436\,\text{kN}} = 0.34\,\text{m}.$$

This is *less* than one-sixth the length of the base ($\frac{1}{6} \times 2.65$ m $=$ 0·44 m) so that the resultant line of action comes *within the middle third* of the base. This is indicated by the arrow in Fig. 6.3. When the resultant comes within the middle third of the base, the whole of the underside of the base is in compression, and there is no tendency for uplift to occur anywhere.

In such a case, the *maximum* pressure on the soil under one end of a foundation of size $L \times B$ is given by the formula

$$q_{max} = \frac{Q}{L \times B}\left(1 + \frac{6e}{L}\right). \qquad (6.10)$$

In our case

$$q_{max} = \frac{436\,\text{kN}}{2\cdot65\,\text{m} \times 1\cdot2\,\text{m}}\left(1 + \frac{6 \times 0\cdot34\,\text{m}}{2\cdot65\,\text{m}}\right)$$

$$= 138\,(1 + 0\cdot765)\,\text{kN/m}^2$$

$$= 243\,\text{kN/m}^2.$$

Similarly, the *minimum* pressure is given by

$$q_{min} = \frac{Q}{L \times B}\left(1 - \frac{6e}{L}\right), \tag{6.11}$$

so that in our case

$$q_{min} = \frac{436\,\text{kN}}{2\cdot65\,\text{m} \times 1\cdot2\,\text{m}}\left(1 - \frac{6 \times 0\cdot34\,\text{m}}{2\cdot65\,\text{m}}\right)$$

$$= 32\,\text{kN/m}^2.$$

These maximum and minimum pressures of $243\,\text{kN/m}^2$ and $32\,\text{kN/m}^2$ are plotted to some suitable scale, as indicated in Fig. 6.3. The pressure distribution under the foundation is then indicated by the straight line joining the two points so plotted.

At the critical section for bending (XX in Fig. 6.3) the pressure may then be calculated or scaled off, and is $148\,\text{kN/m}^2$.

For the reinforced-concrete design the characteristic loads and hence the pressure intensities must be increased by a partial safety factor, which will again be assumed to be $1\cdot5$, to take account of the combination of dead and imposed loads applied to the base.

The bending moment at XX is due to the sum of the rectangular and triangular pressure distributions acting to the left of XX, so that

$$M = (1\cdot2\,\text{m} \times 1\cdot2\,\text{m} \times 148\,\text{kN/m}^2 \times 1\cdot5) \times 0\cdot6\,\text{m}$$

$$+ \left(1\cdot2\,\text{m} \times 1\cdot2\,\text{m} \times \frac{95}{2}\,\text{kN/m}^2 \times 1\cdot5\right) \times 0\cdot8\,\text{m}$$

$$= (192 + 82)\,\text{kN m}$$

$$= 274\,\text{kN m}.$$

Using the Design Chart to determine the reinforcing steel required

$$\frac{M}{bd^2} = \frac{274 \times 10^6}{1200 \times 450^2}\,\text{N/mm}^2$$

$$= 1\cdot13\,\text{N/mm}^2,$$

and from the chart

$$\frac{100A_s}{bd} = 0.32\,;$$

hence

$$A_s = \frac{0.32 \times 1200 \times 450}{100}\ \text{mm}^2$$

$$= 1730\ \text{mm}^2.$$

This is provided by six 20 mm bars (area = 1890 mm²). As M/bd^2 is 1·13, which is less than our maximum value of 3·75 N/mm², we know that the design strength of the concrete will not be exceeded under the ultimate design load.

Independent base, loaded eccentrically, outside middle third

6.11. The eccentricity in the case we have just considered was such that the resultant line of action came within the middle third of the base. Thus there was a positive compression under the full extent of the base; or in other words, q_{min} could never be negative.

Sometimes it happens that the eccentricity is such that the line of action of the resultant comes *outside the middle third.* Then the formulae (6.10) and (6.11) do not apply. The following example will demonstrate the matter.

A column 240 mm × 240 mm carries a total direct load of 300 kN and a bending moment of 300 kN m. The gross bearing capacity of the supporting soil is 250 kN/m², as before.

We shall try a base 3 m × 1·5 m × 600 mm thick, as shown in Fig. 6.4.

Then

column load	300 kN
weight of base	62 kN
total load Q	362 kN.

Therefore the eccentricity is

$$e = \frac{M}{Q} = \frac{300\ \text{kN m}}{362\ \text{kN}} = 0.83\ \text{m}.$$

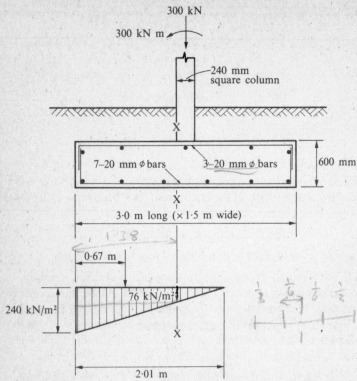

FIG. 6.4. Independent base, loaded eccentrically, outside middle third

This is more than one-sixth the length of the base ($\frac{1}{6} \times 3$ m = 0·5 m), so that the resultant comes outside the middle third and is 0·67 m from the edge of the base, as indicated in Fig. 6.4.

Assuming a triangular distribution of stress, the length of base under pressure is

$$3 \times 0\cdot67 \text{ m} = 2\cdot01 \text{ m},$$

giving an *average* pressure intensity of

$$\frac{362 \text{ kN}}{2\cdot01 \text{ m} \times 1\cdot5 \text{ m}} = 120 \text{ kN/m}^2$$

and a *maximum* edge-pressure of twice this, that is,

$$q_{max} = 2 \times 120 \text{ kN/m}^2 = 240 \text{ kN/m}^2.$$

The pressure distribution is then plotted to some suitable scale, as shown in Fig. 6.4. The pressure at XX is calculated or measured off and is $76\,\text{kN/m}^2$.

To calculate the bending moment at XX the pressure due to the characteristic loads must be multiplied by a partial safety factor which, as previously, we will take as $1\cdot5$.

$$M = (1\cdot38\,\text{m} \times 1\cdot5\,\text{m} \times 76\,\text{kN/m}^2 \times 1\cdot5) \times \frac{1\cdot38\,\text{m}}{2} \ +$$

$$+ \left(1\cdot38\,\text{m} \times 1\cdot5\,\text{m} \times \frac{164}{2}\,\text{kN/m}^2 \times 1\cdot5\right) \times (\tfrac{2}{3} \times 1\cdot38\,\text{m})$$

$$= (163 + 234)\,\text{kN\,m}$$

$$= 397\,\text{kN\,m}.$$

Using the Design Chart to determine the reinforcing steel required

$$\frac{M}{bd^2} = \frac{397 \times 10^6}{1500 \times 550^2}\,\text{N/mm}^2$$

$$= 0\cdot87\,\text{N/mm}^2\,;$$

hence

$$\frac{100\,A_s}{bd} = 0\cdot24$$

and

$$A_s = \frac{0\cdot24 \times 1500 \times 550}{100}\,\text{mm}^2$$

$$= 1980\,\text{mm}^2,$$

which is provided by seven 20 mm diameter bars (area = 2200 mm²).

Because of the pressure distribution indicated in Fig. 6.4 it is clear that the right-hand end of the base is not pressing down on the soil at all, and indeed the weight of this part of the base is being used as a counterweight against an uplifting tendency. In other words, the right-hand end of the base is tending to drop down from the remainder, and for this reason it is advisable to provide a little reinforcement along the top of the base. In the present example three 20 mm diameter bars would be suitable.

When the resultant comes outside the middle third of the base, it is advisable to check what margin the foundation has for stability.

Suppose in our case the eccentricity were increased, by matters beyond our control or knowledge, some 50 per cent, that is, from 0·83 m to 1·25 m. Then the maximum edge-pressure in the soil would be

$$q_{max} = 2 \times \frac{362\,\text{kN}}{3 \times 0 \cdot 25\,\text{m} \times 1 \cdot 5\,\text{m}} = 644\,\text{kN/m}^2.$$

This would be within the *ultimate* capacity of a soil whose *safe* bearing capacity is $250\,\text{kN/m}^2$, so that a reasonable margin for stability is ensured.

A point of interest is that if, in our calculations, we had ignored the self-weight of the base, we should have had an eccentricity of

$$e = \frac{300\,\text{kN m}}{300\,\text{kN}} = 1\,\text{m},$$

giving a maximum edge-pressure of

$$q_{max} = 2 \times \frac{300\,\text{kN}}{(3 \times 0 \cdot 5\,\text{m}) \times 1 \cdot 5\,\text{m}} = 266\,\text{kN/m}^2,$$

as against the $240\,\text{kN/m}^2$ we obtained previously. And strictly this should be related to a net bearing pressure for the soil (without the γz term) which, 600 mm higher up, would be

$$
\begin{aligned}
q_a &= 250 - \gamma z \\
&= 250 - (18 \times 0 \cdot 600)\,\text{kN/m}^2 \\
&= (250 - 11)\,\text{kN/m}^2 \\
&= 239\,\text{kN/m}^2.
\end{aligned}
$$

Clearly then, the more accurate calculation, taking into account the term γz and the self-weight of the base, is well worth doing in cases where eccentric loads have to be considered.

Column strip foundation

6.12. The next type of spread foundation we shall design is a *column strip foundation*. The columns of the building are arranged at 5 m centres in one direction and 7 m centres in the other direction. Each column is 300 mm × 300 mm and carries a concentric load of 900 kN. The safe bearing capacity of the soil is $75\,\text{kN/m}^2$.

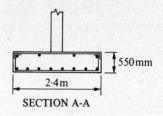

550 mm

2·4 m

SECTION A-A

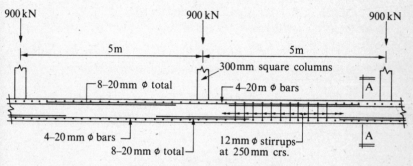

900 kN   900 kN   900 kN

5 m   5 m

300 mm square columns

8–20 mm φ total

4–20 m φ bars

A

4–20 mm φ bars

8–20 mm φ total

12 mm φ stirrups at 250 mm crs.

A

FIG. 6.5. Column strip foundation

If we were to use independent column bases, these would need an area of

$$\frac{900}{75} \text{ m}^2 = 12 \text{ m}^2,$$

requiring a base size of 3·5 m × 3·5 m. For these dimensions, a suitable thickness would be 750 mm, otherwise the deflections would become excessive.

However, with a continuous strip foundation, where we have the greater stiffness arising from reverse bending, a thickness of only 550 mm will suffice, clearly making for a considerable economy in concrete. And, for each column, the perimeter of excavation side requiring timbering or other protection is only 2 × 5 = 10 m, whereas with independent bases it would be 4 × 3·5 = 14 m, 40 per cent more.

The area of base required per column for a strip foundation is 12 m² as before and the minimum width will therefore be

$$\frac{12 \text{ m}^2}{5 \text{ m}} = 2·4 \text{ m}.$$

The longitudinal bending moments in a regular strip foundation of this form, where reverse bending occurs, may be taken approximately as

$$M = \frac{QL}{16}.$$

(6.12)

These bending moments occur under the columns (producing tension in the bottom of the foundation) and midway between the columns (producing tension in the top of the foundation).

Adopting our partial safety factor of 1·5,

$$M = \frac{(900 \times 1 \cdot 5) \times 5}{16} \text{ kN m}$$

$$= 422 \text{ kN m}.$$

Using the Design Chart to determine the area of steel

$$\frac{M}{bd^2} = \frac{(422 \times 10^6)}{2400 \times 485^2} \text{ N/mm}^2$$

$$= 0 \cdot 74 \text{ N/mm}^2;$$

hence

$$\frac{100 A_s}{bd} = 0 \cdot 20$$

and

$$A_s = \frac{0 \cdot 20 \times 2400 \times 485}{100} \text{ mm}^2$$

$$= 2330 \text{ mm}^2.$$

This is provided by four 20 mm diameter bars, lapped as shown in Fig. 6.5 to give eight bars in the bottom of the foundation under the columns and eight bars in the top of the foundation midway between the columns (area of steel at each critical section for bending = 2510 mm^2).

It can be seen that the compressive stress in the concrete corresponding to the ultimate load will not exceed the characteristic strength, as $M/bd^2 = 0 \cdot 74 \text{ N/mm}^2$, which is well below the limiting value of 3·75 N/mm^2.

The transverse bending moment can be calculated using eqn. (6.6), whence

$$M = \frac{QL}{8}$$

$$= \frac{(900 \times 1 \cdot 5) \times 2 \cdot 4}{8} \text{ kN m}$$

$$= 405 \text{ kN m}.$$

The area of steel can be found using the Design Chart:

$$\frac{M}{bd^2} = \frac{405 \times 10^6}{5000 \times 500^2} \text{ N/mm}^2$$

$$= 0 \cdot 32 \text{ N/mm}^2 \,;$$

hence

$$\frac{100 A_s}{bd} = 0 \cdot 09$$

and

$$A_s = \frac{0 \cdot 09 \times 5000 \times 500}{100} \text{ mm}^2$$

$$= 2250 \text{ mm}^2.$$

This is provided by 12 mm diameter stirrups at 250 mm centres (twenty stirrups per 5 m bay giving an area of 2260 mm^2), which serve conveniently to hold the 20 mm top reinforcements in place while the foundation is being concreted.

We check for shear as we did in § 6.8, but in this case, where the foundation is narrow in relation to its length, the shear failure is more likely to occur along planes either side of the column and a distance of $1 \cdot 5 D$ from the faces, where D is the thickness of the base. In our case the critical section is $1 \cdot 5 \times 550$ mm $= 825$ mm from the face of the column.

The width of the section is $2 \cdot 4$ m, and if we assume that the bearing pressure under the foundation is uniform at 75 kN/m^2, then the shear force due to ultimate loads across each critical section can be calculated as

$$V = 2 \cdot 4 \text{ m} \times \{2 \cdot 5 - (0 \cdot 825 + 0 \cdot 15)\} \text{ m} \times 75 \text{ kN/m}^2 \times 1 \cdot 5$$

$$= 412 \text{ kN}.$$

The shear stress is therefore

$$v = \frac{(412 \times 10^3)}{2400 \times 485} \text{ N/mm}^2$$

$$= 0.35 \text{ N/mm}^2,$$

which is equal to the permissible value of 0.35 N/mm^2, and therefore satisfactory.

If a base thickness of 500 mm had been selected in the first instance it would have been found that the shear stress was 0.40 N/mm^2, in which case the slab thickness would have had to be increased to avoid the use of shear reinforcement.

Raft foundation

6.13. Consider now a building with columns arranged at 4 m centres in both directions. The columns are 300 mm × 300 mm and each carries a load of 750 kN. The safe bearing capacity of the ground is 75 kN/m^2 net.

If we were to use independent column bases, these would need an area of

$$\frac{750}{75} \text{ m}^2 = 10 \text{ m}^2,$$

requiring bases 3·2 m × 3·2 m which at 4 m centres would be only 0·8 m apart. This is therefore a case where a *raft foundation* would be the most economical. We shall try a flat slab 500 mm thick, as shown in Fig. 6.6.

Let us design an internal bay of such a flat-plate slab. Bending takes place in two directions at right angles; but for convenience we consider the bending in each direction separately as follows.

As in the previous example the effects of bending will be to produce tension in the bottom of the slab under the columns, and tension in the top of the slab across the line parallel and midway between the columns.

Now the total bending moment per bay in one direction, *producing tension in the bottom of the slab across the line joining the columns,* is

$$M = \frac{QL}{16}. \tag{6.13}$$

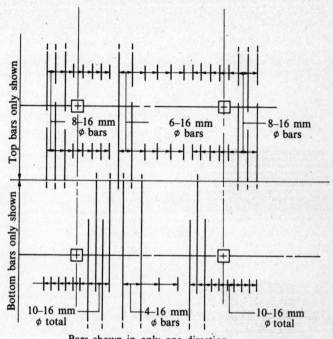

Top bars only shown

Bottom bars only shown

8–16 mm φ bars

6–16 mm φ bars

8–16 mm φ bars

10–16 mm φ total

4–16 mm φ bars

10–16 mm φ total

Bars shown in only one direction
Bars in other direction are similar

PLAN

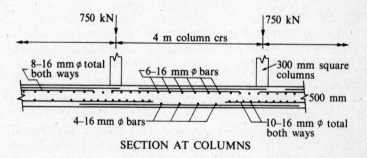

750 kN

750 kN

4 m column crs

8–16 mm φ total
both ways

6–16 mm φ bars

300 mm square
columns

500 mm

4–16 mm φ bars

10–16 mm φ total
both ways

SECTION AT COLUMNS

FIG. 6.6. Raft foundation

Again adopting a partial safety factor of 1·5, this gives in our case

$$M = \frac{(750 \times 1\cdot5) \times 4}{16} \, \text{kN m}$$

$$= 281 \, \text{kN m}.$$

Using the Design Chart to determine the total area of bottom steel required

$$\frac{M}{bd^2} = \frac{281 \times 10^6}{4000 \times 435^2} \, \text{N/mm}^2$$

$$= 0\cdot37 \, \text{N/mm}^2;$$

hence

$$\frac{100 A_s}{bd} = 0\cdot10$$

and

$$A_s = \frac{0\cdot10 \times 4000 \times 435}{100}$$

$$= 1740 \, \text{mm}^2.$$

However, we note from the fact that $100A_s/bd = 0\cdot10$ that the Code of Practice requirement (referred to in § 6.7) that the area of reinforcement should be not less than 0·15 per cent of bd, is not satisfied and we must, therefore, modify the area of steel provided to suit the provision of the Code.

In our case

$$\frac{0\cdot15 \, bd}{100} = \frac{0\cdot15 \times 4000 \times 435}{100} \, \text{mm}^2$$

$$= 2610 \, \text{mm}^2.$$

This area of steel is not distributed uniformly over the total width of the bay since the majority of the bending occurs in the more heavily loaded half-bay width straddling the line of the columns. Therefore across the 2 m width under the columns we provide 75 per cent of the 2610 mm^2 (= 1960 mm^2); and across the remaining 2 m width we provide the balance, being $(2610 - 1960)\,\text{mm}^2 = 650\,\text{mm}^2$. These areas are met respectively by ten 16 mm diameter bars (area = 2010 mm^2) and four 16 mm diameter bars (area = 804 mm^2).

For the bending *producing tension in the top of the slab across the line midway between the columns,* the minimum area of steel of 2610 mm^2 must again be provided. This also is apportioned unequally between the half-bay widths, though not in the same proportions. The 2 m width straddling the column lines takes 55 per cent of the 2610 mm^2 ($= 1435$ mm^2) and the remaining 2 m width has the balance of $(2610 - 1435)$ mm$^2 = 1175$ mm^2. These are met respectively by eight 16 mm diameter bars (area $= 1610$ mm^2) and six 16 mm diameter bars (area $= 1210$ mm^2), giving a total of 2820 mm^2.

In our case, where the columns are spaced at equal intervals in both directions, the amount of bending in the slab will be equal in both directions. Therefore the calculation given above for reinforcement in one direction applies equally for the reinforcement required in the slab in the other direction at right angles.

The reader should now be able to check for himself the shear stress in the raft at the columns.

The above calculation applies strictly only to the internal bays of the raft. At the external bays, the amount of reinforcement may require some adjustment. Sometimes it becomes necessary to increase by about 25 per cent the amount of reinforcement in the top of the raft in the direction at right-angles to the raft edge. This depends on how far the raft projects beyond the lines of the outermost columns, and also on whether the loads in the outer columns are less than the loads in the inner columns — which they frequently are.

It is appropriate to add a word of warning in relation to this procedure for designing raft foundations. Although with firm ground there will be very little deflection of the raft under load, with more compressible soils greater settlements will take place under the columns than under the centres of the panels, causing a redistribution of the moments in the slab.

This does not matter when the columns are laid out in a regular pattern and where the panels between column lines are square or almost so, but it does become important if the column loads are irregularly spaced, or if some loads are very much heavier than others, or where the bays are rectangular and the length of a panel is more than 30 per cent greater than the width. In such cases a design procedure should be used which takes into account the deformation of the ground below the raft.

$\dfrac{M}{bd^2}$ (N/mm²)

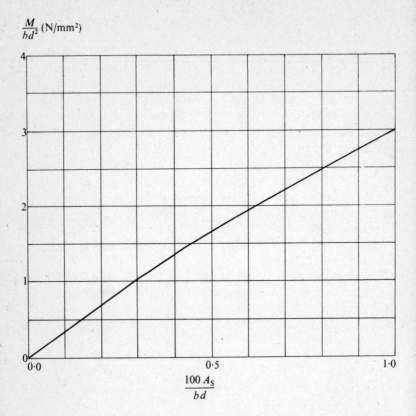

$\dfrac{100\,A_S}{bd}$

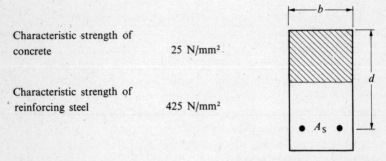

| Characteristic strength of concrete | 25 N/mm² |
| Characteristic strength of reinforcing steel | 425 N/mm² |

DESIGN CHART. Determination of steel percentage using grade 25 concrete and high-yield steel

7

Piled foundations

7.1. Where ground of poor bearing capacity extends down a considerable distance, and a harder stratum is reached at depths of 5 m or more, it usually pays to provide a piled foundation.

Suppose the load in the column in Fig. 7.1 is 2500 kN, the upper stratum to a depth of 10 m is soft clay good for an allowable bearing pressure of 100 kN/m^2, and below this there is a compact well-graded ballast. If this column were to be carried on the upper clay it would require a foundation with an area of 25 m^2, that is, a foundation 5 m square and, say, 1 m thick. The same load, however, could be carried on four piles, each 12 m long, driven down into the ballast so as to

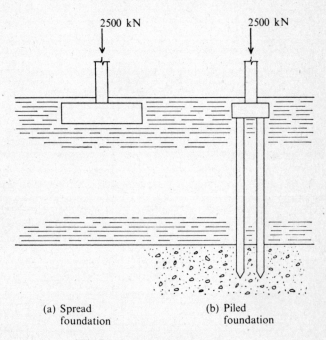

(a) Spread foundation

(b) Piled foundation

FIG. 7.1. Spread and piled foundations

carry 625 kN on each pile; and the load from the column would be transferred to the piles by a pile cap, only 2 m square and 750 mm thick. The advantages of the piled foundation in these circumstances are that it will not settle or deflect appreciably; it occupies considerably less space than a spread foundation, and normally it will be cheaper.

In the previous example, if the allowable bearing pressure on the clay had been only 50 kN/m², the area required for a spread foundation would have been

$$\frac{2500 \text{ kN}}{50 \text{ kN/m}^2} = 50 \text{ m}^2,$$

requiring a foundation about 7 m square. This would have become very expensive. Indeed, if adjacent columns had been closer together than 7 m, a bearing foundation would have been impossible, unless a buoyant foundation were used, which again would increase the cost further.

The further alternative, of excavating 10 m down to the ballast and building up in piers, would almost certainly be ruled out on considerations of cost.

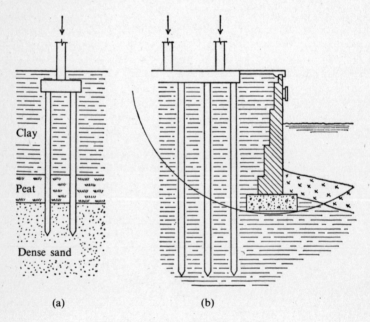

FIG. 7.2. Examples of piled foundations

7.2. Other situations where piled foundations are necessary are indicated in Fig. 7.2.

If a normal spread foundation were used in case (a), the peat layer would squeeze, over a period of time, to perhaps half its original thickness. Therefore piles must be driven through the peat to the sand strata beneath; then no additional load will be imposed on the peat and no reliance placed upon it.

In case (b) the intense loading from the foundations of a new building at the level of an existing wharf would surcharge the wall, tending to push it over into the water. There is also the risk of the far greater vertical loading on one side of the wall causing a cartwheel slip failure as indicated. If piles are driven to well below the level of the wall footing, both these dangers are eliminated.

7.3. Until the early part of this century, piles were generally of timber carefully selected by the engineers, often by visiting the forests. Since then considerable changes have taken place in the types of piles used and it is now common practice for piles to be of concrete, generally reinforced with steel bars, though in some cases precast piles are prestressed using high-tensile steel wire.

In certain special circumstances steel H-section piles may provide the best solution to the engineering problem where the relatively lighter weight for a given load capacity is a significant advantage. This applies when very long piles are required, and in these circumstances, or when considerable variations in length occur owing to undulations in the bearing strata, the ease with which steel piles can be extended by butt-welding, or shortened using an oxyacetylene torch, can be of considerable importance. For structures such as jetties, where the piles have to project well above ground level in their final situation, steel piles (frequently these are hollow boxes of square or hexagonal cross section) may show a considerable advantage. In these difficult construction situations the robust character of the steel piles may make them preferable to the precast concrete alternative.

It must be emphasized, having made reference to other types of structure, that the majority of piles are used to support building foundations or foundations for industrial works, and for such purposes the concrete pile is normally the most economical type to use. These can be either *cast-in-situ* by placing concrete in a shaft previously formed in the ground in the required position, or *precast* and subsequently driven into the ground.

Cast-*in-situ* piles

7.4. Cast-*in-situ* piles are formed in a variety of ways by different specialist firms. Generally they are considered in two categories, the smaller-diameter piles with diameters between 300 mm and 600 mm and the larger-diameter piles over 600 mm. Depending upon their size and the type of ground, small-diameter piles can be used to carry loads up to about 1000 kN and can support considerably greater loads than this if they are used in groups.

There are occasions when very heavy column loads from an especially tall building or an unusually heavy piece of plant may require a larger number of smaller-diameter piles to support them than can conveniently be fitted under the foundation. It is possible, particularly when there is a firm founding stratum at a reasonable depth, that large-diameter piles would provide a suitable and economical solution to this problem, supporting, as they do in the most favourable conditions, loads up to 20 000 kN on a single shaft. The design of such piles often involves under-reaming (enlarging the diameter of the bottom section of the pile to increase its bearing capacity). The engineering considerations which are involved in judging the advisability of the use of large-diameter piles are such that they are beyond the scope of a simple book.

We shall, therefore, concentrate our attention on the smaller-diameter *in-situ* piles, the two main types being as follows:

1. *Driven cast-in-situ piles* are formed by driving a tube, with a closed end, into the soil until the required depth or resistance is achieved. Concrete is then poured into this tube, which may or may not be removed depending upon the system being employed.

2. *Bored cast-in-situ piles* are formed by boring into the ground, and then using a steel tube, which follows down behind the boring tools, to act as a liner to prevent the ground collapsing. Concrete is poured into this tube which is withdrawn as the concreting proceeds.

The basic difference between these two types of piles is that in the first case the soil is *displaced* laterally by the driving of the tube, and with the second type the soil is *removed* during the boring operation.

In both cases after the shaft has been formed, whether by *driving* or by *boring*, a cage of reinforcement is lowered into the tube before the shaft is fillled with concrete. With some systems the concrete is vibrated or hammered as the tube is lifted. This ensures that the concrete flows outwards to fill the hole made by the tube, together with any voids at the sides of the shaft where soft pockets or porous materials may exist in the ground.

Cast-*in-situ* piles have advantages over precast piles in that they can be constructed immediately following the placing of a contract, without the delay necessary for the manufacture and curing of precast piles. In addition, it is not necessary to know exactly the lengths required for the piles, as the tube can be taken down until the required stratum is reached, and then just sufficient concrete placed as will fill the shaft up to the required level. Thus the construction of cast-*in-situ* piles can be started more quickly than precast piles, and in certain circumstances there is a greater economy of materials.

Another advantage of cast-*in-situ* piles is that with certain proprietary systems it is possible to construct the piles to very considerable depths. Thus the authors have used piles 35 m long penetrating silty clay to get support on hard boulder clay beneath. Precast piles of this length would have been impracticable due to the difficulties of handling and driving.

Bored piles have the advantage of causing very little vibration to the surrounding ground or nearby structures; they are formed quite simply by using a three-legged rig only about 4 m high, whereas driven piles normally require a special pile-driving frame of height varying from about 10 m to 20 m or more, depending on the length of pile required. Thus bored piles can be constructed more easily on sites where access is restricted; and although the work of boring may go more slowly than with piles that are driven, it may be cheaper to use bored piles on small jobs where only a few piles are required. Bored piles do, however, have two main disadvantages compared with driven piles. First, the very act of driving piles tightens the soil particles and creates a wedging action on the pile; but with bored piles, this advantage is lost because the shaft is formed in the ground after the soil has been bored out. Secondly, the driving-resistance of driven piles can give some indication of the load-carrying capacity of the finished piles; but with bored piles no evidence of this kind is available.

Disadvantages common to all forms of cast-*in-situ* piles are as follows. It is difficult to ensure that the reinforcement is held everywhere in the centre of the pile, so that the protection of the reinforcements against corrosion is uncertain. And in grounds of a soft and plastic nature, there is a risk that the ground in the lower layers may squeeze into the concrete before it has hardened, and in this way reduce the effective cross-sectional area of the pile. Another objection is that certain soils are liable to attack young concrete, particularly if it is not thoroughly compacted.

Precast piles do not suffer these unfortunate features: the reinforcements and concrete are placed above ground level in moulds of precise dimensions under fully controlled conditions, and the piles are not driven into the ground until the concrete is well matured.

Various systems for forming *in-situ* driven and bored piles are shown in Figs. 7.3–7.5 from which the reader will be able to understand the main stages involved in the construction.

The Simplex Standard Pile (Fig. 7.3) is formed by driving into the ground a hollow steel tube, usually 400 mm or 450 mm diameter, fitted with a double-rimmed cast-iron shoe. The joint between the tube and the shoe is made watertight by the insertion of packing. The tube is driven by drop-hammer until the required penetration or set is obtained. The hammer and drive cap are then lifted away, a cage of reinforcement lowered into the tube, and the tube filled with concrete to the

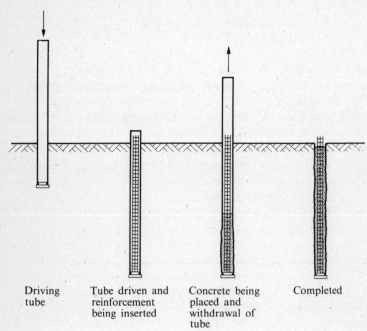

| Driving tube | Tube driven and reinforcement being inserted | Concrete being placed and withdrawal of tube | Completed |

FIG. 7.3. Typical cast-*in-situ* driven pile

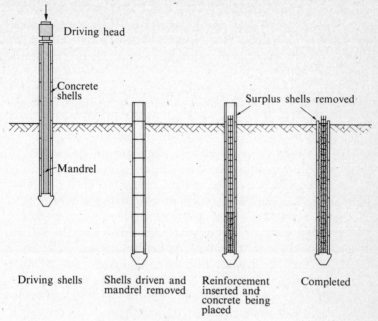

Driving head

Concrete
shells

Surplus shells removed

Mandrel

| Driving shells | Shells driven and mandrel removed | Reinforcement inserted and concrete being placed | Completed |

FIG. 7.4. West's shell-driven pile

required level. The tube is then slowly withdrawn. During the process of withdrawal, the concrete, being fairly fluid, issues from the lower end of the tube, and is forced downwards and outwards by its own weight, filling the hole made by the tube together with any voids in the sides of the hole which may have been formed through displacement of stones or boulders during the driving operation.

The West's Driven Pile (Fig. 7.4) is formed by threading reinforced-concrete tubes on to a steel mandrel with a solid concrete shoe. The joints between the shells are made with steel bands which fit into recesses at the ends of the shells, the joint being treated with a bituminous mastic sealer. The whole of the tube, mandrel, and shoe is driven into the ground until the required set is obtained. The hammer blow is delivered direct on to the shoe by means of the steel mandrel. Simultaneously a cushioned blow is applied to the shells, through a special arrangement on the mandrel driving head, causing the shells to follow the shoe. When the required set is obtained the steel mandrel is withdrawn, leaving the shoe and concrete tube in position. A cage of reinforcements is then lowered into the hollow pile formed by the concrete shells, and the pile filled with concrete. The advantages of this method are that there is no risk of variation in cross-section of the pile, and there is no risk of contamination of the core concrete due to impurities in the ground, as the cast-*in-situ* core is protected by the precast shell.

The normal bored pile (Fig. 7.5) is still widely used because it can be constructed with a simple tripod rig which is both light and compact and can, therefore, be transported cheaply and used on sites without the need to provide expensively prepared access roads and working areas. Because the boring operations are only mildly percussive such piles can be formed adjacent to existing buildings or services without damage, and the compact design of the equipment make it possible to pile in areas where headroom is very restricted. Indeed, certain specialist firms have tripod rigs which can be used to construct piles inside buildings with no more than the normal headroom. The piles are formed by first making a boring, the hole being lined with steel tubes as the boring proceeds to keep the hole open or to seal off the ground-water. The steel tubes are sunk in the ground either by their own weight or by lightly tapping with a suitable tool. When the steel tube has been sunk to the required level, a small amount of concrete is placed in the bottom and compacted by dropping a ram on it. A cage of reinforcement is then lowered into the tube and further batches of concrete are deposited and rammed in stages. The lining tubes are

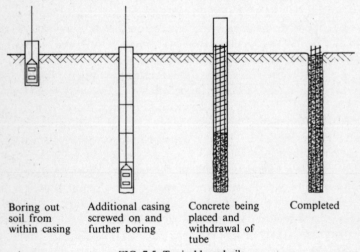

Boring out soil from within casing

Additional casing screwed on and further boring

Concrete being placed and withdrawal of tube

Completed

FIG. 7.5. Typical bored pile

slowly extracted as concreting proceeds until the pile has been formed to the required finished level.

With all cast-*in-situ* piles it is important to concrete the shaft to a level approximately 0·5 m above the final cut-off level to enable the top weak concrete to be removed, thus ensuring only concrete of adequate strength remains in the pile.

Precast piles

7.5. Typical precast piles are shown in Fig. 7.6. Precast piles do not suffer many of the unfortunate features to which *in-situ* piles are susceptible, as the reinforcements and concrete are placed above ground

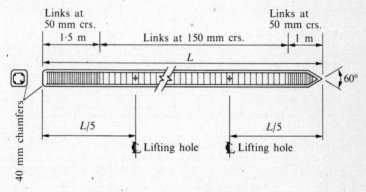

Pile size (mm square)	Normal maximum working load (kN)
250	300
300	400
350	500
400	700
450	900

Pile length (m)	Recommended minimum size (mm)	Minimum reinforcement	
		Main rods (number × dia)	Links (dia. × crs.)
7	250	4 × 20 mm	6 mm at 150 mm
10	300	4 × 20 mm	
13	350	4 × 25 mm	
16	400	4 × 32 mm	8 mm at 150 mm
19	450	4 × 32 mm	

FIG. 7.6. Details of precast piles

level in clean moulds of precise dimensions under fully controlled conditions ensuring a high quality of construction. Furthermore, the piles are not driven into the ground until the concrete is well matured, and when they are driven the effect of the striking hammer is a greater test of strength than the piles will subsequently have to endure in carrying their permanent applied loads; in this way, any faults in the manufacture of the piles are shown up in the driving, so that the finished piles are, in a sense, each pre-tested.

In handling and transporting precast piles it is important that they should be lifted only at their fifth points, as shown in Fig. 7.7, otherwise

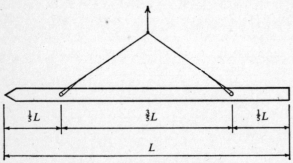

FIG. 7.7. Slinging of precast piles

the piles are likely to be damaged. If the piles are not lifted as shown, they would have to be constructed of stouter proportions, which would greatly increase their cost as well as their weight and the difficulty of handling and driving.

The efficiency of pile-driving depends on the relation between the weight of the pile and the weight of the hammer, so that the lighter the pile the more efficiently it is driven. This is a practical point in favour of cast-*in-situ* driven piles, where the weight of the steel tube is much less than the weight of a precast concrete pile and, therefore, lighter equipment, with its better mobility, can be used to form piles of this type.

End-bearing and friction piles

7.6. Some piles are driven or formed through soft ground to derive most of their support by bearing on a harder stratum such as ballast or rock lower down. These piles are known as *end-bearing piles*.

Other piles are used in circumstances where no well-defined hard layer can be reached at any reasonable depth, and these piles rely for support on side resistance over a considerable proportion of their length. These piles are known as *friction piles*.

Often, in practice, piles are supported by a combination of the two effects.

The load-bearing capacity of end-bearing piles driven down to ballast or sand can generally be forecast within reasonable limits of accuracy by pile-driving formulae as given later. But the carrying capacity of friction piles in clays and silts cannot be determined reliably in the same way; and it is preferable, in these cases, either to rely on calculations on the frictional resistance between the ground and the pile, or, much better, to apply test loads to a number of the piles some while after they have been completed.

Test piles

7.7. Where a single site involves the sinking of a large number of piles it is advisable to construct a few full-scale test-piles under normal

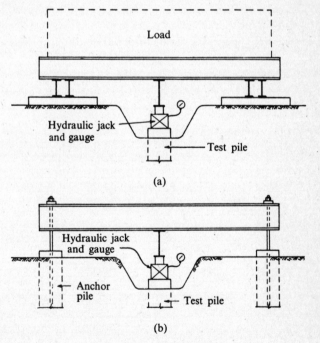

(a)

(b)

FIG. 7.8. Test-loading of piles

working conditions. Loading tests on such piles give a better indication of the carrying capacity of the works piles than any form of calculation.

Piles can be load-tested in one of two ways, as indicated in Fig. 7.8. The first method is to support a suitable mass of pig-iron or concrete blocks on a simple bridge of steel beams, and to load the pile by jacking down from the undersides of the beams. This method has the disadvantage of the cost of bringing in and building up the load on the steel beams. The second method is to avoid the provision of any special mass for providing the load, but to tie down to other piles constructed in the ground nearby. Often four such anchor piles will be sufficient for the purpose of tailing down the load necessary for testing one pile.

While the test load is being built up, in stages, to the full amount, measurements of the depression of the head of the pile are taken with great care, using either a surveyor's level, or, preferably, a gauge clamped to a long beam supported from the ground well away from the areas affected by the pile movement.

The ultimate resistance of works piles is most satisfactorily determined by actual tests to failure of test piles in this way. The likely ultimate resistance of other piles on the same site can then be estimated by comparing (in the case of driven piles) their resistance to driving, or (in the case of bored piles) the nature of the strata through which they are bored.

A word of warning. Test piles tell you the resistance of a single pile, which will stress the ground in the manner indicated in Fig. 7.9(a).

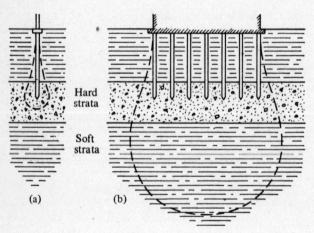

FIG. 7.9. Limitation of load-testing piles

However, where many piles under a large building or structure are all
loaded at the same time; the stressed zone in the ground extends to a
greater depth below the bottoms of the piles as indicated in Fig. 7.9.(b);
and if there should be a soft soil layer at this greater depth, *the group
of piles* would suffer, whereas the *single pile* would not be affected.
For this reason test borings should always be made on every piling site
to seek out any soft layers, and clearly these borings should extend
well beyond the depth intended for the piles.

   Another instance where a large group of piles may carry less total
load than the sum of the single piles is where short frictional piles
compete with one another for support from the same plan area of soil,
and only the piles at the perimeter of the group can get adequate

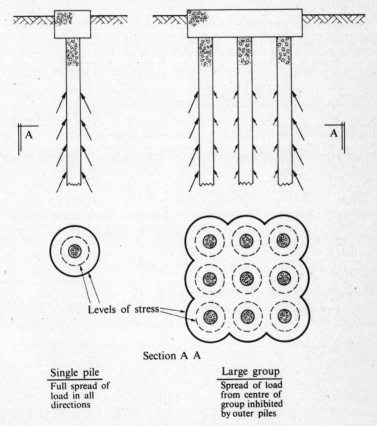

Section A A

Single pile	Large group
Full spread of load in all directions	Spread of load from centre of group inhibited by outer piles

FIG. 7.10. Ground over-piled with short frictional piles

spread to enable them to approach anywhere near the value of the load-carrying capacity of a single pile (see Fig. 7.10).

Piles designed on the basis of test loads should normally be tested to twice the load they are required to carry as their safe working duty. On the other hand, where reliance is placed on a good pile-driving formula (see § 7.11) a load factor of $2\frac{1}{2}$—3 is suitable for end-bearing piles driven to ballast or sand, but a higher factor is necessary for piles in clays or silts.

Bearing capacity of piles on basis of soil tests

7.8. The bearing capacity of piles driven in cohesive soils cannot be reliably determined by the use of any pile-driving formula. There are three main reasons for this.

First, the sideways shake of the pile, as it is being driven, makes an enlarged hole so that the pile derives little frictional support at the time of driving — yet over a period of some weeks this gap will close in as the clay squeezes home and holds snugly against the pile. Secondly, moisture, trapped temporarily in the quickness of the driving process, may lubricate the sides of the pile — yet in time this water will percolate away, allowing the full adhesive strength to develop between the clay and the pile. Both these considerations will make for poor sets, giving the appearance of an unrealistically low bearing capacity for the pile.

The third confusion is due to a deceptively high end-resistance arising from the low permeability of the soil building up short-term pressures at the instant of impact. Such pressures will dissipate after the effect of driving but, of course, are always present to cause confusion at the actual moment of striking.

For these reasons the ultimate bearing capacity of piles driven in cohesive soils has to be determined either by test-loading (as described in § 7.7) or by calculation based on the shear strengths of the soils. Shear-strength calculations, furthermore, are the only means of assessing the bearing capacity of bored piles, where clearly no driving data will exist. Calculation under these circumstances is carried out as follows.

The ultimate bearing capacity of the pile will be

$$Q_f = Q_f' + Q_f'', \tag{7.1}$$

where Q_f' = the ultimate *end-bearing* capacity
and Q_f'' = the ultimate *side-friction* capacity.

And if

A_p = the cross-sectional area of the pile (m²)
o = the surface area of the pile per unit length (m²/m)
l = the length of the pile in the soil (m)
c = cohesion of the soil (kN/m²),

then we have

$$Q_f' = 9A_p c \qquad (7.2)$$

and $$Q_f'' = 0.5\, loc. \qquad (7.3)$$

Eqn. (7.2) is nothing more than eqn. (4.6), with N_c taken as 9. Eqn. (7.3) is nothing more than the shear strength of the soil acting on the surface area of the pile and multiplied by a factor of 0·5 to allow for the adhesion between the disturbed soil and the pile being less efficient than the full internal shear strength of the soil itself.

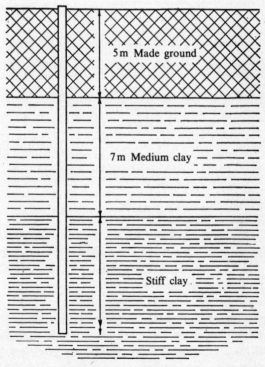

FIG. 7.11. Example of bored pile through various strata

7.9. As an example of this soil-mechanics approach, consider the bored pile shown in Fig. 7.11. The strata consist of 5 m of made ground, underlain by 7 m of medium clay ($c = 50\,kN/m^2$) and underlain again by stiff clay ($c = 200\,kN/m^2$). The pile is required to support a working load of 400 kN. We will try a pile 400 mm diameter and 18 m long.

From eqn. (7.2) we have

$$Q_f' = 9 \times \left(\frac{\pi \times 400^2}{4 \times 10^6}\right) \times 200 = 226\,kN.$$

From eqn. (7.3), we have for the upper clay

$$Q_f'' = 0{\cdot}5 \times 7 \times \frac{\pi 400}{10^3} \times 50 = 220\,kN.$$

Similarly, we have for the lower clay

$$Q_f'' = 0{\cdot}5 \times 6 \times \frac{\pi 400}{10^3} \times 200 = 754\,kN.$$

Therefore total ultimate bearing capacity $Q_f = \underline{1200\,kN.}$

With the actual load to be carried of 400 kN, the load factor would be

$$F = \frac{1200}{400} = 3$$

which would be satisfactory for a pile in stiff clay calculated in this manner.

Negative skin friction

7.10. In the example given in § 7.9, we have tacitly assumed that the made ground has no strength or ability to provide support for the pile and lies idle making no contribution one way or the other. This may be true if the made ground has been in position for a considerable period of time and is unlikely to move or settle further as a result of disturbance or other subsequent influences.

However, if for any reason the internal shear strength of the made ground is interfered with (and the very construction of our piles may produce such interference) the made ground may tend to settle in relation to the underlying clay layers; and in such a situation the pile, with its support from beneath, will resist such downward tendency, and the made ground will produce a *negative skin friction* on the pile — the pile actually seeking to support the made ground.

In this way the downward load on the pile will become greater than allowed for in the calculation, and this may have the effect of overcoming the shear resistance of the pile lower down in the clay layers, causing the pile to settle. This may prove to be only a temporary condition, lasting over a matter of months or a year until the made ground has regained its adjusted form of compaction and equilibrium.

Piles constructed through upper layers of soft sensitive clays are likely to behave in much the same way, producing negative skin friction on piles that gain their support lower down.

Pile-driving formulae

7.11. All pile-driving formulae are based on the assumption that the bearing capacity of a pile under static conditions bears a simple relationship to its resistance to driving for the last metre or so.

This is obviously a little irrational. It largely ignores the nature of the ground through which the pile was driven to get down to its finished level. It takes very little account of the effect of friction on the sides of the pile, and this friction tends only to develop later on as the ground settles back against the pile over a period of some weeks. And of course there can be no appreciation of any soft layer in the ground below the toes of the piles.

Thus no pile-driving formulae should be used without also considering the findings of a soil investigation along the lines already described in Chapters 4 and 5. And no pile-driving formula will give information as good as an actual load-test on a finished pile.

Nevertheless, pile-driving formulae do give some guidance, provided the limitations of the formulae are realised. We may use the following notation:

R = the ultimate driving-resistance of the pile (kN),
W = the weight of the hammer (kN),
h = the height of drop of the hammer (mm),
s = the final set of the pile per blow (mm).

Then from considerations of kinetic energy

$$W \times h = R \times s$$

so that

$$R = \frac{Wh}{s} \text{ kN.} \tag{7.4}$$

In practice this equation is found to be far too great a simplification of the matter. It ignores the energy losses involved in the temporary elastic compression of the pile and the helmet and the packing, the temporary compression of the ground, and also the bouncing of the hammer on the pile. If it were not for these losses, the pile would penetrate into the ground some distance greater than s.

Thus a very much more rational formula was developed by Hiley in 1925 as follows:

$$R = \frac{Wh}{s + c/2} \eta \text{ kN,} \qquad (7.5)$$

where c = the sum of the temporary elastic compressions in the pile, packings, and ground (mm),

and η = the efficiency of the blow of the hammer

$$= \frac{(W + Pe^2)}{(W + P)},$$

where P = the weight of the pile, helmet, etc. (kN),

e = the coefficient of restitution of the materials under impact.

The temporary compression in the pile and ground are found by actual measurements made while the pile is being driven, and the temporary compression of various forms of packing has now been established experimentally by laboratory tests. These values are given in various engineering manuals.

This may all seem rather a complicated mathematical treatment to apply to anything as unrefined as the driving of concrete limbs weighing about 50 kN, with a 30 kN hammer, through 20 m or more of variable geological strata.

A second piling formula worthy of note is due to Oscar Faber, and expressed as follows:

$$R = \frac{W\left(h - \dfrac{d}{7}\right)}{s + xh} \text{ kN,} \qquad (7.6)$$

where d = the diameter of the pile (mm),

x = a factor depending on the length and elastic moduli of the pile and any packings.

Faber found that generally x has a value not greatly different from 0·02; so that, by ignoring the small term $d/7$, we arrive at a simplified version of eqn. (7.6) as follows:

$$R = \frac{Wh}{s + 0·02\,h} \text{ kN.} \qquad (7.7)$$

The merits of Faber's formula are that, over a lifetime's experience, he found that his calculated values agreed more closely with the results of actual pile tests than any other formula he knew; and, requiring no reference to tables for constants, the simplified version gives a ready tool for quick and simple calculation.

No pile-driving formula can be regarded in any sense as scientifically accurate. Many reasons for this have been given earlier. Under these circumstances, probably the simple Faber formula, given in eqn. (7.7), provides as reliable an estimate of the ultimate resistance of a driven pile as any other formula.

7.12. As an example of the use of a pile-driving formula, consider the piles 12 m long shown in Fig. 7.1. Piles driven into frictional soils such as ballast are better suited to calculation based on pile-driving formulae than piles driven into cohesive soils; and, in such a case, a load factor of $2\frac{1}{2}$ would be adequate using any of the formulae given in eqns. (7.5), (7.6), or (7.7).

Suppose the piles were driven with a 30 kN hammer, dropping 1·5 m until a final set was reached of five blows per 25 mm of penetration. Then using eqn. (7.7) we have

$$R = \frac{Wh}{s + 0·02\,h}$$

$$= \frac{30 \times 1·5 \times 10^3}{5 + (0·02 \times 1·5 \times 10^3)} \text{ kN}$$

$$= 1290 \text{ kN.}$$

This would be the ultimate resistance of each pile. As the actual load to be carried per pile is 500 kN, the load factor would be

$$R = \frac{1290}{500} = 2\frac{1}{2},$$

which would be satisfactory.

Pile caps

7.13. Referring back to Fig. 7.1, it will be noted how the load from the superstructure column is transferred to the four piles by means of a *pile cap*. The pile cap has to be designed so as to be strong enough not to fail by bending at the middle. A check has also to be made that the shear stresses at the column and at the piles are not excessive; though frequently the thickness selected to give the required stiffness, and to give adequate anchorage for the column and pile reinforcements, leads to fairly low shear stresses in the concrete.

A suitable detail for the pile cap would be as indicated in Fig. 7.12. The piles are at 1·1 m centres in both directions, and the pile cap is 2 m square and 750 mm thick.

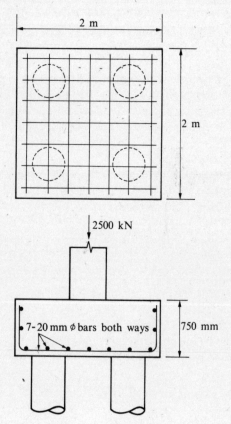

FIG. 7.12. Pile cap over four piles

In a case like this, where the foundation is bending in two directions at right-angles between four points of support, the ultimate design bending moment across the cap in any direction may be taken approximately as

$$M = \frac{QL}{8}.$$ (7.8)

Then, in our case, using our partial safety factor of 1·5,

$$\dot{M} = \frac{(2500\,\text{kN} \times 1·5) \times 1·1\,\text{m}}{8}$$

$$= 515\,\text{kN m},$$

and the area of steel can be determined using the Design Chart.

$$\frac{M}{bd^2} = \frac{515 \times 10^6}{2000 \times 670^2}\,\text{N/mm}^2$$

$$= 0·57\,\text{N/mm}^2,$$

hence

$$\frac{100A_s}{bd} = 0·16$$

and

$$A_s = \frac{0·16 \times 2000 \times 670}{100}\,\text{mm}^2$$

$$= 2140\,\text{mm}^2,$$

which is provided by seven 20 mm bars (area 2200 mm²) in both directions.

In this case, the load from the column will spread directly onto the piles, so there is no possibility of shear failure.

8

Retaining walls

8.1. Excavations in rock can be finished to a vertical face so that the rock stands sheer for a considerable height. Soils behave differently and cannot stand more steeply than their natural angle of repose. This frequently is inconvenient (as, for example, in certain rail and road cuttings or in basements to buildings), and then it becomes necessary to construct a retaining wall behind which the soil will stand, supported artificially by leaning against the back of the wall.

8.2. In designing retaining walls we are faced with four inter-related problems. First, we have to estimate what forces will be created on the back of the wall by the soil which is to be retained. Next, we have to select a suitable profile for the wall and its base, and determine whether the wall will be stable so as not to fail by overturning. Then we have to check whether the bearing pressure under the base is suitable and whether the base is deep enough to prevent the wall sliding forward. And finally we have to analyse the wall itself in terms of reinforcement required and stresses in the concrete.

These stages each require a certain amount of experience. This applies particularly to the choice of wall profile which can be determined only by a process of trial and correction.

Before attempting to give any mathematical formulae for determining the lateral pressures which can act on retaining walls, it is perhaps better to appreciate from a commonsense approach the likely limits over which these pressures can vary. We shall also consider to what extent these pressures can be controlled by simple design features, such as drainage precautions and the like.

Active pressures

8.3. A stiff clay can be excavated to a vertical face and will stand like this for quite a while, depending on its moisture content and other physical properties. However, on exposure to the effects of drying air,

122

the clay will lose its cohesive nature and will crumble. On the other hand, an excess of moisture will so weaken the clay that it slumps almost like a liquid.

Suppose the liquid clay were entirely without shear strength; then it would produce a hydrostatic pressure of γz, where

γ = the bulk density of the soil,
and z = the depth below surface level.

If we take the bulk density of the liquefied clay as $1500\,\text{kg/m}^3$, which for convenience in making our calculations we shall express as $15\,\text{kN/m}^3$, this would give us a lateral pressure of $15\,z\,\text{kN/m}^2$. Clays which are more dense than this are sufficiently plastic to develop internal shear forces.

Thus, the maximum *active* lateral pressure from a liquid clay, acting at depth z below the surface level, would be $p_a = 15z$, but clays which are stiffer so as to be in the plastic range generally press very much less, and it is then frequently assumed that the active pressure is $p_a = 5z$ kN/m^2.

When back-filling clays behind retaining walls it is important to ensure that the material is not deposited in large chunks in a dry state, as in this condition it will be very difficult to compact into a homogeneous mass, and active pressures even above $15z\,\text{kN/m}^2$ could then occur. However, proper attention to the construction procedures on site should avoid this problem.

Now consider a sand. In its dry state this will stand as a heap at an angle of repose of about $30°$. If we now fill with dry sand the space between this heap and the back of our retaining wall (Fig. 8.1), it is

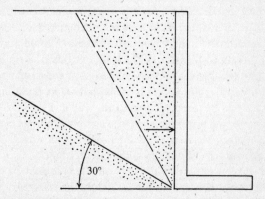

FIG. 8.1. Sand pressing on back of retaining wall

clear that half the additional sand will press against the back of the wall and half will press on top of the original heap. Thus *one-third* of the weight of the dry sand is active against the wall, or approximately $15/3 \, \text{kN/m}^3$, so that $p_a = 5z \, \text{kN/m}^2$.

Suppose, now, the sand were saturated by filling behind the wall with water. Then the pressure on the wall would be increased by the hydrostatic pressure of the water, so that the total active pressure would be $p_a = 5z + 10z = 15z$.

Thus we see that the practical limits for the active pressures behind retaining walls, whether from clays or sands, will come within the range of about

$$p_a = 5z \, \text{kN/m}^2 \text{ to } p_a = 15z \, \text{kN/m}^2. \tag{8.1}$$

It is true that hard clays may stand for a time so as to produce no active pressure at all, but no engineer would dare to rely on this as a basis for designing a permanent wall.

Water pressure

8.4. The point arises now as to whether the soil should be regarded as dry ($p_a = 5z$) or saturated ($p_a = 15z$). Where proper drainage facilities are provided, and build-up of water pressure cannot occur, it is safe to design for active pressures of $p_a = 5z$.

However, such drainage facilities are sometimes impracticable, as for example in certain cases of basements or pits. In these situations it must be assumed that with cohesionless soils, which allow water to pass through them freely, the water pressure will act on the walls for the full depth below the level of the water table, and p_a should be taken as $15z$ below this level. In the case of clay the matter becomes more difficult to assess. It can be argued that if the wall is constructed hard against an excavated clay face the imperviousness of the clay should prevent water ever finding its way to the back of the wall, but this is an optimistic view and should not be relied on in practical design. Indeed, owing to the impervious nature of the clay soil, it is likely that where no drainage can be provided water will be trapped between the wall and the clay face, and so, whatever level the water table may be assumed to be at elsewhere on the site, in designing retaining walls the possibility of water pressure right up to ground level should be taken into account.

However, for a truly impervious clay one thing is clear. When the water gets between the clay and the wall, only the water can press on the wall — not the water plus the clay. Alternatively, if the condition of the clay is such that its active pressure p_a is greater than $10z$, then the clay will push the water away, and only the active pressure of the clay need be taken into account in the design calculations.

Drainage

8.5. Normally it is possible for engineers to provide suitable drainage facilities at retaining walls to prevent, or at any rate to limit, the possible build-up of water pressure. This may not be so with basements or pits, but generally is so for free-standing retaining walls, as shown in Fig. 8.2.

Drainage material placed behind the back of the wall will prevent the build-up of water, which can then be run away through weepholes or by a longitudinal back-drain to suitable outlet points. Water from weepholes should be collected, or run away, so as to prevent the soil under the toe of the base being softened. Back-drains should be built over a continuous concrete filling to prevent the water running down to foundation level where it could seep underneath and lubricate the base and so set off a sliding failure.

In cohesive soils it may be worth giving umbrella protection to the soil at the back of the wall by concrete paving laid to falls to drainage gulleys.

Where an extensive hillside behind the back of a wall is likely to give a considerable run-off of surface water, this water should be intercepted by a continuous drainage ditch dug in the hillside behind the wall. To prevent the water, cut off by this ditch, seeping down into the soil and acting on the back of the retaining wall, the ditch should be kept away from the wall a distance at least equal to the wall height.

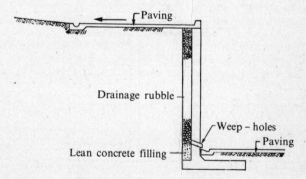

FIG. 8.2. Drainage at retaining wall

Surcharge

8.6. The pressures given in eqn (8.1) are due only to the ground behind the wall, and assume that this is finished off to a horizontal surface. However, when the ground is built up at a slope, or where imposed loadings occur on top of the ground, the pressures on the back of the wall will be increased quite considerably, and we have to take account of this in our calculations.

Common examples of imposed loadings behind retaining walls are the storage of goods at a wharf or loading platform, or traffic at the top of a cutting or on the approaches to a bridge. The effect of such imposed loading may conveniently be considered as equivalent to an extra depth of soil behind the wall. Thus, in Fig. 8.3, if

w = the imposed load on the ground behind the wall (kN/m^2),
γ = the bulk density of the soil (kN/m^3),
z_x = the equivalent extra depth of soil (m),

we have

$$z_x = \frac{w}{\gamma}. \qquad (8.2)$$

The extra pressure due to z_x may then be determined by using the simple eqn (8.1) or (with caution) the more elegant formulae given later in eqns (8.3) or (8.4).

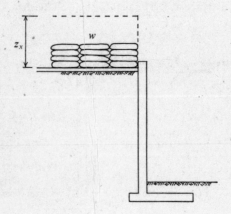

FIG. 8.3. Surcharge of retaining wall

Mathematical theories for pressures on walls

8.7. While not greatly favouring the application of soil-mechanics formulae to calculations of lateral pressures on retaining walls, the authors feel it right to include here an indication of these formulae. First we shall consider the *active pressure* pushing on the back of the wall. Later we shall consider the *passive pressure* at the front which prevents the wall from being pushed forwards.

(a) *Active pressure*

In §4.3 we discussed at length Coulomb's general equation for the relationship between shear strength, cohesion, and friction in soils. This equation is

$$s = c + p \tan \phi.$$

We saw also, in Fig. 5.4, how this equation can be represented for the condition at failure by a line drawn as a tangent to the Mohr semicircles. Now, mathematically, it can be shown quite simply that if

p_1 = the major stress, acting *vertically*,

and

p_3 = the *horizontal* stress,

then

$$p_3 = p_1 \tan^2 \left(45° - \frac{\phi}{2} \right) - 2c \tan \left(45° - \frac{\phi}{2} \right).$$

And since here $p_1 = \gamma z$, we have the *active horizontal pressure* on the back of the wall equal to

$$p_a = \gamma z \tan^2 \left(45° - \frac{\phi}{2} \right) - 2c \tan \left(45° - \frac{\phi}{2} \right). \tag{8.3}$$

This formula was first published by Bell.

For cohesionless soils, where $c = 0$, the second term on the right-hand side becomes zero, so that

$$p_a = \gamma z \tan^2 \left(45 - \frac{\phi}{2} \right). \tag{8.4}$$

This special case of the formula is generally attributed to Rankine. By a little mathematical manipulation this may be re-written (for those who prefer it) as

$$p_a = \gamma z \left(\frac{1 - \sin \phi}{1 + \sin \phi} \right). \tag{8.5}$$

Either equation (8.4) or (8.5) will give the same numerical result, and for truly cohesionless soils may be regarded as giving realistic results. Frequently these will be of the order of $p_a = 5z$, as derived in eqn (8.1) for dry sands.

For cohesive soils eqn (8.3) will give *negative* pressure values down to a certain minimum depth; this is based on the cohesive strength enabling the soil to stand sheer but, as already explained, it would be imprudent to rely on this in any design calculations. Accordingly, sound as it may be theoretically, eqn (8.3) needs tempering with a little commonsense, particularly over the range of the smaller depth values.

(b) *Passive pressure*

Now we must consider the *passive pressure*, at the front of the wall foundation, which prevents the wall being pushed forward.

The lateral pressure required to move a soil forward is very much greater than the active pressure a soil will exert on the back of a wall. Thus *passive pressures* are many times greater than *active pressures*. Therefore to calculate what passive resistance we can rely upon at the front of a retaining wall, we need to derive fresh formulae.

Turning again to Coulomb's equation and Fig. 5.4, it can be demonstrated mathematically that if

p_1 = the major stress, acting *horizontally*,

and

p_3 = the *vertical* stress,

then

$$p_1 = p_3 \tan^2 \left(45° + \frac{\phi}{2} \right) + 2c \tan \left(45° + \frac{\phi}{2} \right).$$

Putting $p_3 = \gamma z$, we have the *passive horizontal pressure* at the front of the wall equal to

$$p_p = \gamma z \tan^2 \left(45° + \frac{\phi}{2} \right) + 2c \tan \left(45° + \frac{\phi}{2} \right). \tag{8.6}$$

This formula is also due to Bell.

For cohesionless soils, where $c = 0$, the second term on the right-hand side becomes zero, so that

$$p_p = \gamma z \tan^2 \left(45° + \frac{\phi}{2}\right). \tag{8.7}$$

This is Rankine's formula for passive pressure, and may also be expressed

$$p_p = \gamma z \left(\frac{1 + \sin \phi}{1 - \sin \phi}\right). \tag{8.8}$$

Eqns (8.7) and (8.8) are both reasonably reliable for use with truly cohesionless soils. Eqn (8.6), however, needs using with a great deal of care, particularly as passive resistance is normally sought at relatively shallow depths where cohesive soils are liable to shrink away from their duty as a result of seasonal drying out.

Modes of failure of retaining walls

(a) *Failure by rotation*

8.8. It is indicated at Fig. 8.4 (a) how the total active force P on the back of a free-standing wall combines vectorially with the weight of the wall to produce an inclined resultant thrust R. If this resultant comes beyond the width of the base, the wall will fail by immediate overturning.

If, on the other hand, the resultant thrust comes well in from the edge of the base, and the base is of suitable width, the wall will be stable against rotation. However, it is necessary to check that the maximum

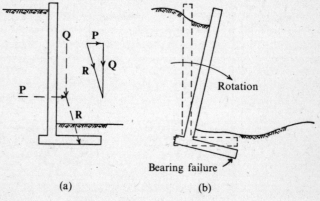

(a)   (b)

FIG. 8.4. Failure of wall by rotation

bearing pressure under the toe of the base does not exceed the *safe bearing capacity* of the soil, much as we did for eccentrically loaded foundations in §§6.10 and 6.11, otherwise the toe will settle and the wall will fail by rotation in this way (see Fig. 8.4(b)).

Generally, in designing retaining walls of this type, the resultant thrust comes outside the width of the middle third. This does not matter. But it is necessary in all problems of stability such as this to check that there is a *margin of stability* of at least $1\frac{1}{2}$ on the *ultimate bearing capacity* of the soil, just as we did in the worked example in §6.11. In other words, it is not sufficient to design the wall for stability with the normal assessment of the active pressure behind the wall, and check that the safe bearing capacity of the soil under the toe of the wall is not exceeded; it is *also* necessary to check that a 50 per cent increase of the active pressure will not cause failure by the ultimate bearing capacity of the soil being exceeded.

(b) *Failure by forward movement*

Two things prevent a free-standing wall from moving forward — the passive resistance of the soil at the front of the base, and the friction between the soil and the underside of the base (see Fig. 8.5(a)).

The method of calculating the passive resistance — and the uncertainty of this in the case of cohesive soils — have already been described in §8.7(b). Where a considerable passive resistance is required this is often best achieved by constructing a projecting key under the base of the wall, near the heel, as shown in Fig. 8.5(b).

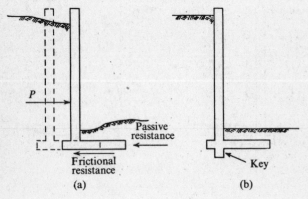

FIG. 8.5. Failure of wall by forward movement

The base friction on cohesionless soils (sands and gravels) can be taken as

$$R_f = Q \tan \phi. \tag{8.9}$$

On cohesive soils the base friction is calculated as

$$R_f = cL, \tag{8.10}$$

where L is the length of the base under pressure. c is, of course, the cohesion of the soil; normally this is limited in eqn (8.10) to about 50 kN/m^2, because at this point the *adhesion* between the clay and the concrete becomes the limiting factor, no matter what the actual shear strength of the clay may be.

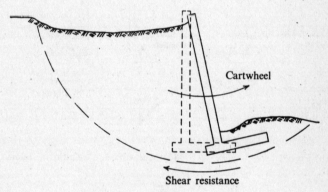

FIG. 8.6. Cartwheel failure of wall

(c) *Cartwheel failure*

Failure by cartwheel action may occur in poor strength non-frictional soils, as indicated in Fig. 8.6. Here it is not the soil immediately at the wall which fails, but a much larger mass of soil which fails and carries the wall with it.

The disturbing influence in this case is the weight of ground behind the wall causing a greater moment about some centre of rotation than the weight of ground in front of the wall acting in combination with the shear resistance of the soil along the arc of failure.

The method of analysis follows the same procedure as already outlined in §4.11.

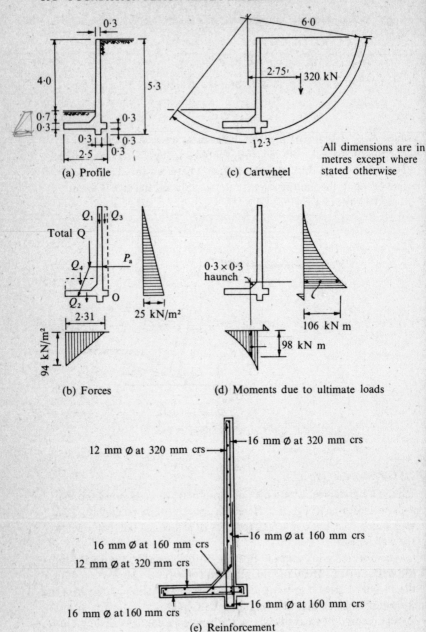

(a) Profile

(c) Cartwheel

All dimensions are in metres except where stated otherwise

(b) Forces

(d) Moments due to ultimate loads

(e) Reinforcement

FIG. 8.7. Retaining wall with base in front

Wall with base in front

8.9. As a practical example of retaining-wall design, consider the problem indicated at Fig. 8.7(a). A wall is required to hold back 4 m of clay at the side of a new cutting. The cohesive strength of the clay is 50 kN/m^2 and its bulk density is 20 kN/m^3.

For this purpose a profile is chosen with the base extending from the front face of the wall (compare this with the different arrangement in Fig. 8.8). The advantages of the present arrangement are (1) that we do not have to excavate the soil situated to the right of the wall, with consequent saving of cost, and (2) the clay to the right is undisturbed, and not so likely to lead to any great build-up of water pressure.

With care, the 300 mm horizontal heel projection can be cut into the vertical clay face; and this heel greatly enhances the stability of the wall, giving a useful tailing-down effect with a leverage arm of greatest advantage.

For convenience, the whole of the calculation is made for a vertical slice of the wall 1 m wide.

(a) *Stability*

The forces acting on the structure are indicated in Fig. 8.7, and the calculation is most conveniently set out in tabular fashion as shown in Table 8.1:

TABLE 8.1

	Forces		Arm about O (m)	Anticlockwise moment about O (kN m)
	Vertical (kN)	Horizontal (kN)		
Q_1 (wall)	36·0	—	0·45	16·2
Q_2 (base)	18·0	—	1·25	22·5
Q_3 (soil over heel)	28·2	—	0·15	4·2
Q_4 (soil over base)	26·6	—	1·55	41·2
P_a (soil)	—	62·5	1·67	104·4
Total forces	108·8	62·5	—	—
Total moment	—	—	—	188·5

The vertical loads are each worked out by multiplying the cross-sectional area shown in the diagram by the unit weight of the material. Thus the weight of the concrete base, for example, is

$$Q_2 = 2·5\,m \times 0·3\,m \times 24\,kN/m^3 = 18·0\,kN \text{ per metre of wall.}$$

For the soil weights, the unit weight is taken as $20 \, \text{kN/m}^3$, so that, for example,

$$Q_3 = 4{\cdot}7 \, \text{m} \times 0{\cdot}3 \, \text{m} \times 20 \, \text{kN/m}^3 = 28{\cdot}2 \, \text{kN per metre of wall.}$$

The active horizontal pressure on the back of the wall is taken from eqn (8.1) as $p_a = 5z$. Therefore at 5 m depth the pressure will be

$$p_a = 5 \times 5 \, \text{kN/m}^2 = 25 \, \text{kN/m}^2,$$

and this will reduce up the wall to zero pressure at the top. With a *triangular distribution* of pressure like this the total active force on the back of the wall will be

$$P_a = \frac{25 \, \text{kN/m}^2 \times 5 \, \text{m}}{2} = 62{\cdot}5 \, \text{kN per metre of wall,}$$

and this will act at a point one-third of the way up the 5 m triangle, that is, $1{\cdot}67$ m above the point marked O in the diagram.

Now we take moments of all these applied forces (vertical and horizontal) about any centre, here chosen for convenience at O. The arm about which each of the forces acts is indicated in Table 8.1; the last column gives the moment, being the product of each force and its respective lever arm. Thus the total *anti-clockwise* moment is $188{\cdot}5$ kN m.

Now for equilibrium this moment has to be balanced by an equal and opposite mament of $188{\cdot}5$ kN m acting in a *clockwise* sense. This clockwise moment will comprise the product of the vertical reaction R_v under the base and the distance x of its line of action from the same centre O. We know that R_v must equal the sum of all the applied vertical forces Q_1, Q_2, Q_3, and Q_4. Therefore

$$R_v \times x = 188{\cdot}5,$$

so that $$x = \frac{188{\cdot}5}{108{\cdot}8} = 1{\cdot}73 \, \text{m.}$$

Thus R_v is a distance $(2{\cdot}50 - 1{\cdot}73) = 0{\cdot}77$ m from the toe of the base, and clearly outside the middle third. Assuming a triangular distribution of stress under the base (as we did in §6.11), the length of base under pressure is $3 \times 0{\cdot}77$ m $= 2{\cdot}31$ m, giving an *average* pressure of

$$\frac{108{\cdot}8}{2{\cdot}31} \, \text{kN/m}^2 = 47 \, \text{kN/m}^2$$

and a *maximum* edge-pressure of $2 \times 47 \, \text{kN/m}^2 = 94 \, \text{kN/m}^2$.

For our clay of $c = 50\,\text{kN/m}^2$, the safe bearing capacity from eqn (4.13) is

$$q_a = \frac{cN_c}{F} + \gamma z.$$

In our case we can take N_c as 6.

Then
$$q_a = \frac{50 \times 6}{3} + (20 \times 1\cdot0)\,\text{kN/m}^2$$

$$= (100 + 20)\,\text{kN/m}^2$$

$$= 120\,\text{kN/m}^2.$$

The maximum edge-pressure of $94\,\text{kN/m}^2$ is therefore satisfactory.

Note that if the active force on the back of the wall were increased by 50 per cent, the anti-clockwise moment would become $241\,\text{kN m}$, so that x would be $241/108\cdot8\,\text{m} = 2\cdot22\,\text{m}$. Thus R_v would be $(2\cdot5 - 2\cdot22)\,\text{m} = 0\cdot28\,\text{m}$ from the toe of the base. Then the average pressure under the base would be $108\cdot8/0\cdot84\,\text{kN/m}^2 = 130\,\text{kN/m}^2$, and the maximum edge-pressure would be $260\,\text{kN/m}^2$. The ultimate capacity of the clay, from eqn (4.9) is

$$q_f = (50 \times 6) + (20 \times 1\cdot0)\,\text{kN/m}^2$$

$$= (300 + 20)\,\text{kN/m}^2$$

$$= 320\,\text{kN/m}^2,$$

so there is an adequate margin of stability.

In practice, before R_v could get as near to the toe as $0\cdot28\,\text{m}$, the heel of the base would try to rise very slightly, and in doing this would have to lift a far greater weight of clay than we took in the calculation for Q_3, actually spreading back from the face of the wall at about $30°$. Thus the margin of stability is greater than has been indicated above.

(b) Forward movement

The total active horizontal force P_a is $62\cdot5\,\text{kN}$. This has to be resisted by the passive resistance of the soil, plus the friction under the base.

With clay it would be unwise to rely on the passive resistance of the ground in front of the base, owing to seasonal shrinkage. However, the ground in front of the key is better protected, and deeper, so that we can safely allow for this in our calculation. Then, from eqn (8.6) we have the passive horizontal pressure

$$p_p = \gamma z \, \tan^2 \left(45° + \frac{\phi}{2}\right) + 2c \tan \left(45° + \frac{\phi}{2}\right).$$

But for a non-frictional clay soil, $\phi =$ zero, so $\tan \left(45° + \dfrac{\phi}{2}\right) = 1$.

Therefore, for a key of depth t,

$$
\begin{aligned}
P_p &= (\gamma z + 2c) \times t \\
&= \{(20 \text{ kN/m}^3 \times 1 \cdot 15 \text{ m}) + (2 \times 50 \text{ kN/m}^2)\} \times 0 \cdot 3 \text{ m} \\
&= (23 + 100) \times 0 \cdot 3 \text{ kN} \qquad\qquad = 36 \cdot 9 \text{ kN.}
\end{aligned}
$$

The base friction force, from eqn (8.10), is

$$R_f = cL$$

$$= 50 \times (3 \times 0 \cdot 77) \text{ kN} \qquad = \underline{115 \cdot 5 \text{ kN.}}$$

Therefore the total resistance to forward movement $\qquad = \underline{152 \cdot 4 \text{ kN.}}$

Thus the factor of safety against forward movement is

$$F = \frac{152 \cdot 4}{62 \cdot 5} = 2 \cdot 4,$$

and this is adequate.

(c) Cartwheel failure

The circle associated with the least factor of safety (or the highest shear stress in the clay) is indicated in Fig. 8.7. The out-of-balance weight of soil tending to cause rotation is 320 kN acting at a distance of 2·75 m to the right of the centre of rotation. This tendency is resisted by the shear stress in the soil, along the arc 12·3 m long, acting at a radius of 6·0 m from the centre of rotation.

Thus 320 kN × 2·75 m = 12·3 m × 6·0 m × shear stress. Therefore, the actual shear stress is

$$\frac{320 \times 2 \cdot 75}{12 \cdot 3 \times 6 \cdot 0} \text{ kN/m}^2 = 12 \text{ kN/m}^2.$$

Thus the factor of safety against cartwheel failure is

$$F = \frac{50}{12} = 4 \cdot 2,$$

which is satisfactory.

(d) *Reinforced-concrete design*

The maximum bending stresses in the wall will occur at the top of the haunch. Here $p_a = 5 \times 4 \cdot 4 \, \text{kN/m}^2 = 22 \, \text{kN/m}^2$, so that the total horizontal force above the haunch causing bending is $\frac{1}{2} (22 \times 4 \cdot 4) = 48 \cdot 4 \, \text{kN}$ per metre run of wall.

Applying our partial safety factor of $1 \cdot 5$ to determine the ultimate design load, our bending moment is therefore

$$M = (48 \cdot 4 \times 1 \cdot 5) \times \frac{4 \cdot 4}{3} \, \text{kN m} = 106 \, \text{kN m}.$$

The area of reinforcing steel is calculated as previously:

$$\frac{M}{bd^2} = \frac{(106 \times 10^6)}{10^3 \times 250^2} = 1 \cdot 7 \, \text{N/mm}^2.$$

From the Design Chart

$$\frac{100 A_s}{bd} = 0 \cdot 49$$

and

$$A_s = \frac{0 \cdot 49 \times 10^3 \times 250}{100} \, \text{mm}^2/\text{m} = 1230 \, \text{mm}^2 \text{ per metre of wall}.$$

This is provided by 16 mm diameter bars at 160 mm centres (area = 1260 mm^2). Higher up the wall, the bending moment reduces rapidly as shown in Fig. 8.7(d), so that part-way up we can stop half the bars, leaving 16 mm at 320 mm centres (see Fig. 8.7(e)).

At the top of the haunch $M/bd^2 = 1 \cdot 7 \, \text{N/mm}^2$, which is less than $3 \cdot 75 \, \text{N/mm}^2$ (see §6.8), and the compressive stress in the concrete is therefore satisfactory.

The concrete shear stress is given by

$$v = \frac{V}{bd} = \frac{(48 \cdot 4 \times 1 \cdot 5) \times 10^3}{10^3 \times 250} = 0 \cdot 29 \, \text{N/mm}^2,$$

which is also satisfactory.

The base is analysed in much the same way as the wall. The maximum bending stresses occur at the left edge of the haunch. We have already calculated the pressure distribution under the base, and this is indicated at Fig. 8.7(b). The bending moment at the haunch due to the pressure is therefore

$$(1 \cdot 6 \, \text{m} \times 29 \, \text{kN/m}^2) \times 0 \cdot 8 \, \text{m}$$

$$+ 1 \cdot 6 \, \text{m} \times \frac{65 \, \text{kN/m}^2}{2} \times 1 \cdot 07 \, \text{m}$$

$$= (37 \cdot 1 + 55 \cdot 6) \, \text{kN m} \qquad = 92 \cdot 7 \, \text{kN m.}$$

This is partially opposed by the bending moment due to the self-weight of the base, and the soil over, namely,

$$1 \cdot 6 \, \text{m} \times \{(0 \cdot 7 \, \text{m} \times 20 \, \text{kN/m}^3) + (0 \cdot 3 \, \text{m} \times 24 \, \text{kN/m}^3)\} \times 0 \cdot 8 \, \text{m}$$

$$= 1 \cdot 6 \, \text{m} \times 21 \cdot 2 \, \text{kN/m}^2 \times 0 \cdot 8 \, \text{m} \qquad = \underline{27 \cdot 1 \, \text{kN m}}$$

giving a net bending moment at the base haunch $\quad = \underline{65 \cdot 6 \, \text{kN m.}}$

This must be increased by our partial safety factor of $1 \cdot 5$ to 98 kN m, which is slightly less than the bending moment we calculated for the wall, and it is satisfactory to run the same reinforcements from the wall round the corner and along the base (see Fig. 8.7(e)). Half the reinforcements are stopped part-way along, where the bending moment has reduced sufficiently.

The shear force at the base haunch due to underside pressure is

$$1 \cdot 6 \, \text{m} \times 29 \, \text{kN/m}^2 \qquad = 46 \cdot 4 \, \text{kN}$$

$$1 \cdot 6 \, \text{m} \times \frac{65 \, \text{kN/m}^2}{2} \qquad = 52 \cdot 0 \, \text{kN}$$
$$= 98 \cdot 4 \, \text{kN}$$

less that due to self-weight and soil over

$$1 \cdot 6 \, \text{m} \times 21 \cdot 2 \, \text{kN/m}^2 \qquad = 33 \cdot 9 \, \text{kN}$$
$$\underline{64 \cdot 5 \, \text{kN.}}$$

Applying the partial safety factor of $1 \cdot 5$, the concrete shear stress is therefore

$$v = \frac{64 \cdot 5 \times 1 \cdot 5 \times 10^3}{10^3 \times 250} = 0 \cdot 39 \, \text{N/mm}^2,$$

which is satisfactory for our concrete with the percentage of tensile steel required.

Wall with base behind

8.10. Consider now the wall indicated in Fig. 8.8. This is required to retain 6 m of dry sand fill where the ground is to be built up, as might be required to provide car-parking facilities in front of an hotel building constructed on a site sloping down to the sea-front. The sand weighs 18 kN/m^3 and has an angle of internal friction of $35°$. The design of the wall is to cater for a uniform imposed surcharge loading of 10 kN/m^2.

In this case it is convenient to build the wall with its base on the side where the material is to be filled. The weight of the fill then gives enhanced stability against rotation and increases the friction under the base against forward movement. Thus the base at Fig. 8.8 is shorter in proportion to the base in Fig. 8.7, and consequently cheaper.

(a) Stability

With frictional soils we can reasonably rely on the mathematical equation (8.5) for determining the active horizontal pressure on the back of the wall. In our case this yields

$$p_a = \gamma z \left(\frac{1 - \sin \phi}{1 + \sin \phi} \right)$$

$$= 18z \left(\frac{1 - 0.574}{1 + 0.574} \right) \text{ kN/m}^2$$

$$= 4.9z \text{ kN/m}^2.$$

It is seen that this is not far from our approximate formula of $p_a = 5z$ derived in eqn (8.1) for a dry sand.

The surcharge of 10 kN/m^2 is equivalent to

$$z_x = \frac{10}{18} \text{ m} = 0.56 \text{ m of soil.} \qquad \text{See eqn (8.2)}$$

This will produce a uniform pressure, extending the full height on the back of the wall, of $p_a = 4.9 \times 0.56 \text{ kN/m}^2 = 2.74 \text{ kN/m}^2$; and a total force on 7 m height of wall of $7 \text{ m} \times 2.74 \text{ kN/m}^2 = 19.2 \text{ kN}$ per metre width.

The active pressure from the soil will vary from zero at the top to $4.9 \times 7 \text{ kN/m}^2 = 34.3 \text{ kN/m}^2$ at 7 m depth, giving a total force on the back of the wall of $34.3 \times \frac{7}{2} \text{ kN} = 120 \text{ kN}$ per metre width.

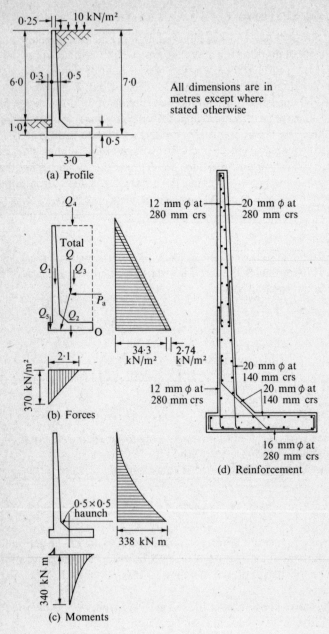

(a) Profile

All dimensions are in metres except where stated otherwise

(b) Forces

(c) Moments

(d) Reinforcement

FIG. 8.8. Retaining wall with base behind

The stability of the wall is then checked in tabular fashion (see Table 8.2) as in the previous example.

TABLE 8.2

| | Forces | | Arm about O (m) | Anticlockwise moment about O (kN m) |
	Vertical (kN)	Horizontal (kN)		
Q_1 (wall)	58·5	—	2·51	146·8
Q_2 (base)	36·0	—	1·50	54·0
Q_3 (soil over base)	272·0	—	1·16	315·5
Q_4 (surcharge)	24·5	—	1·23	30·1
Q_5 (soil over toe)	2·7	—	2·85	7·7
P_a (soil)	—	120·0	2·33	279·6
(surcharge)	—	19·2	3·50	67·2
Total forces	393·7	139·2	—	—
Total moment	—	—	—	900·9

The distance x of the line of vertical reaction R_v from O is therefore

$$x = \frac{900 \cdot 9}{393 \cdot 7} \, \text{m} = 2 \cdot 29 \, \text{m}.$$

This is 0·71 m from the edge of the base so that the average intensity of pressure is $393 \cdot 7/(3 \times 0 \cdot 710) \, \text{kN/m}^2 = 185 \, \text{kN/m}^2$, and the maximum edge-pressure is $2 \times 185 \, \text{kN/m}^2 = 370 \, \text{kN/m}^2$. This would be acceptable.

(b) *Forward movement*

The total active horizontal force P_a is 139·2 kN. The base friction force, using eqn (8.9) is

$$R_f = Q \tan \phi$$
$$= 393 \cdot 7 \times 0 \cdot 7 \, \text{kN}$$
$$= 276 \, \text{kN}.$$

The factor of safety against forward movement, relying only on the base friction is, therefore,

$$F = \frac{276}{139} = 2,$$

indicating that no key under the base is required in this case.

(c) *Cartwheel failure*

There is no risk of cartwheel failure with a good frictional soil of this nature. The reader can readily check this for himself.

(d) *Reinforced-concrete design*

At the top of the wall-haunch the pressure due to the soil will be $4 \cdot 9 \times 6 \, \text{kN/m}^3 = 29 \cdot 4 \, \text{kN/m}^3$, giving a total force above this level of

$$\frac{(29 \cdot 4 \times 6)}{2} \, \text{kN} = 88 \cdot 2 \, \text{kN}.$$

The total force at this level due to surcharge will be $6 \times 2 \cdot 74 \, \text{kN} = 16 \cdot 4 \, \text{kN}$.

Applying the partial safety factor of $1 \cdot 5$ to both these forces to determine the bending moment due to the ultimate load, we have

$$M = \frac{(88 \cdot 2 \, \text{kN} \times 1 \cdot 5) \times 6 \, \text{m}}{3} + \frac{(16 \cdot 4 \, \text{kN} \times 1 \cdot 5) \times 6 \, \text{m}}{2}$$

$$= (264 \cdot 6 + 73 \cdot 8) \, \text{kN m}$$

$$= 338 \cdot 4 \, \text{kN m},$$

and

$$\frac{M}{bd^2} = \frac{338 \cdot 4 \times 10^6}{10^3 \times 450^2} \, \text{N/mm}^2$$

$$= 1 \cdot 7 \, \text{N/mm}^2.$$

From the Design Chart

$$\frac{100A_s}{bd} = 0 \cdot 49,$$

and the area of steel required is

$$A_s = \frac{0 \cdot 49 \times 10^3 \times 450}{100} \, \text{mm}^2$$

$$= 2210 \, \text{mm}^2,$$

which is provided by 20 mm diameter bars at 140 mm centres (area $= 2250 \, \text{mm}^2$) which are stopped off in stages up the height of the wall as in the previous example.

As M/bd^2 has been calculated and found to be $1 \cdot 7 \, \text{N/mm}^2$, which is less than the allowable value of $3 \cdot 75 \, \text{N/mm}^2$, we know that the concrete compressive stress is satisfactory, but a check must also be made on the shear stress at the level of the haunch,

$$v = \frac{V}{bd} = \left\{ \frac{(88\cdot2 \times 1\cdot5) + (16\cdot4 \times 1\cdot5)}{10^3 \times 450} \right\} \times 10^3 \text{ N/mm}^2$$

$$= \frac{(132 + 25)}{450} \text{ N/mm}^2$$

$$= 0\cdot35 \text{ N/mm}^2,$$

which is also satisfactory.

9

Materials and constuction

9.1. Having shown how the type and size of foundations may be
selected to suit the ground conditions, and how the concrete reinforcements may be determined, we can refer here to the materials that
should be used for the reinforced-concrete work and to what precautions should be taken in the construction.

If proper care is taken in the choice of materials and in the construction of reinforced-concrete foundations, the work may be as near
permanent as normal commercial conditions are likely to require.
However, poor materials and poor workmanship can lead to early
deterioration and failure of the foundations, no matter how carefully
and successfully the designs may have been prepared.

9.2. For long life, concrete needs to be dense, with a complete absence
of porosity, voids, and honeycombing.

To achieve dense concrete, a number of requirements have to be met.
The aggregates have themselves to be impervious. They have also to be
suitably graded from the largest size of stones down to the smallest.
Sufficient cement has to be used in the mix to cover the surface of
every aggregate particle. And sufficient water has to be added to set off
the chemical reaction which causes the cement to set and harden, and
also to lubricate the aggregate particles so that they can be properly
compacted to ensure a complete absence of voids.

A surplus of water makes for very weak concrete; and indeed the
strength of concrete depends more than anything else on the ratio
between the water and cement used in the mix. The higher the proportion of water the weaker the mix, and the higher the proportion of
cement the stronger the mix. As the cement and the water both assist
in lubricating the aggregate particles to enable the concrete to be
properly compacted, it is a matter of some judgement to know how
much of the lubrication should be achieved by the use of cement and
how much by the use of water. Clearly, cement is expensive, while
water is cheap.

The compaction of the particles is greatly facilitated if these are of a round nature as found with natural gravels and shingles. Angular particles which are obtained by crushing massive rocks such as limestone or granite are the most difficult to compact, and consequently require greater lubrication to achieve an equal degree of compaction and permanence. Thus rounded aggregates, or irregular near-round aggregates, make for concretes which are more easily compacted for a given amount of cement, and therefore lend themselves to well-compacted, durable concrete at the least cost.

This, of course, would not be true if we were working in an area where crushed stone was readily available in the locality and could be delivered cheaply, whereas rounded aggregates could be procured only by transporting them a considerable distance, perhaps 100 km or more. In this event, it might well be cheaper to use the angular aggregate with the expense of additional cement.

Nowadays, on all but the smallest jobs it is normal to compact the concrete using vibrating tools. This cuts down on manual labour and enables the concrete to be compacted with less water; and since the strength of the concrete depends almost entirely on the water/cement ratio, it enables the amount of cement to be reduced as well. Thus, in skilled hands, the cost of vibrating equipment is repaid in saving of manpower and saving of cement.

9.3. For normal work the most suitable mix of concrete is Grade 25, having a characteristic strength of 25 N/mm^2. Depending on the size of the job and the experience of the contractor, this strength of concrete will be obtained either by specifying a *prescribed mix* which can be selected from the *Code of practice for the structural use of concrete* (CP 110) or by calling upon the contractor to produce a *designed mix*, in which case he will be required to carry out the necessary design and preliminary testing to ensure that the proportions of aggregate, cement, and water which he wishes to use will give the specified strength.

A typical prescribed mix for Grade 25 concrete, which would be suitable for foundation work, would have materials in the ratio of 400 kg of cement, 200 kg of water, 650 kg of sand, and 1200 kg of coarse aggregate having a nominal maximum size of 20 mm. These figures give the weight of dry sand and coarse aggregate and would need to be modified if wet materials were used, so as to take account of the water in the aggregate, but the total quantity of water included in the mix would be retained at 200 kg. For all but the very smallest jobs the constituents of the concrete, with the possible exception of the water, should be measured (or batched) by weight.

The mix described, which would produce approximately 1 m³ of hardened concrete, is a convenient one for sites where 50 kg bags of cement are being used, the quantities of each material being scaled down to suit a concrete mixer having a smaller capacity.

A useful practical test for controlling on site the amount of water required in the mix is the *slump test*. This test, which measures the *workability* of the concrete, is made using an open-ended metal former like a loud-hailer, being a frustum of a cone 300 mm high, 200 mm bottom diameter, and 100 mm top diameter. The former is stood with its base on a steel plate and filled with the concrete to be tested, the concrete being thoroughly compacted by tamping with a steel rod. The cone is then immediately lifted carefully upwards, so that the concrete in the cone slumps under its own weight. The amount the concrete reduces in height from the original 300 mm is known as the *slump* of the concrete.

The prescribed mix, for which proportions have already been given in this section, should have a slump of between 25 mm and 75 mm, and this should be satisfactory for all foundations and retaining walls. Where vibrators are used, concrete with an average slump at the lower end of this range is suitable, especially in foundations without a lot of reinforcement. Concrete with a zero slump has so little water that for outside work it is generally unsatisfactory and leads to imperfect compaction of the materials. Concrete with a 150 mm slump is so runny as to lead to segregation of the materials, leakage of grout through the formwork, and consequent honeycombing and great weakness of the concrete.

9.4. For normal foundation work one would use Ordinary Portland cement of the slow-setting variety. Most cement-works in Great Britain grind their Ordinary Portland cement so fine today that for most foundation work there is no benefit to be achieved in using Rapid-hardening Portland cement.

To ensure adequate durability of the foundations, which are likely to be continuously damp and may well have to withstand freezing and thawing from time to time, it is prudent never to use less than 300 kg of cement in every cubic metre of compacted concrete, even though such cement content may not be required to provide the characteristic strength of 25 N/mm².

Certain soils, particularly clays, are liable to contain sulphates in such a form as will attack concrete made with Ordinary Portland cement. Ordinary Portland cement is satisfactory where the sulphate concentrations are not greater than 0·5 per cent in the soil, or 100 parts in 100 000 parts of ground-water. Beyond this it is necessary to use Sulphate-resisting Portland cement, which is satisfactory for sulphate concentrations up to 2 per cent in the soil or 500 parts in 100 000 parts of ground-water. Wherever there are sulphate conditions, it is wise to adopt a cement content of at least 400 kg per cubic metre of compacted concrete.

However, whichever cements and concrete mixtures are used, the results will be satisfactory only if the concrete is properly compacted, as already discussed in § 9.2. It is the sulphate solutions in the ground-water which destroy the cement by percolating through the concrete, and successful permanent work is only achieved by making the concrete so dense that ground-solutions cannot find their way into the concrete with sufficient freedom to enable the sulphate concentrations to renew themselves readily for further attack.

9.5. The setting and hardening of concrete is the result of a chemical reaction between the cement and the water. When the water is first mixed in with the other ingredients, the cement particles are never wetted right through, owing to the very large surface area they present in relation to their minute weight. But over a period of several weeks the excess water in the mix will work its way through into the core of each individual cement particle, in this way completing the hardening process and so increasing the strength of the concrete. However, if at any stage in the hardening process the concrete is allowed to dry out completely, a hard crust forms at the outer part of the cement particles for as far as these have already been wetted, and this crust prevents further chemical action taking place later, if the concrete is subsequently wetted.

Therefore it is of the greatest importance to ensure that concrete is not allowed to dry out in the early stages of its life. This is particularly so for the first 10–14 days, over which period the concrete should be kept covered with sacking or other proprietary materials which retain the concrete in a wet condition. This wetting of the concrete after the time of the setting of the cement (generally 10 hours or less from the time water was first added to the mix) in no way retards the process of hardening since, as has already been explained, this latter is a chemical process and has nothing to do with any drying-out of the concrete.

9.6. What does very much affect the rate at which concrete achieves its strength is the temperature. Concrete will harden twice as quickly at 15 °C as it will at 2 °C, and the hardening process is almost completely checked when the temperature drops much below freezing.

For this reason concrete should never be placed when the air temperature is below 2 °C. And for practical, speedy work, where shuttering has to be removed with the least possible delay, it is normally advisable to heat the concrete materials to a temperature of 15 °C whenever the air temperature is below 5 °C.

Once the chemical process of the cement-setting has started, the reaction will generate its own heat. Where the concrete is 0·5 m thick or more, this heat will be sufficient to assist in the rate of hardening of the concrete, especially if the concrete is covered with straw, sacking, or other blanketing to retain the heat which is being generated. However, with very thin concrete members, severely exposed to the effects of rain and wind, the heat generated by the chemical reaction is dissipated to such an extent as to be ineffective in this regard. Special attention has then to be given to heating the materials and protecting the finished work from frost attack.

9.7. Until about 10 years ago it was generally more economical to use mild steel in foundations, as high-tensile steel was considerably more expensive and there was no benefit to be gained from the smaller concrete section which could be employed, as concrete stresses are normally low in this type of construction. However, nowadays there is less difference between the price of high-tensile steel and mild steel, and so with good design, where the additional strength can be fully utilized, it makes sense to use high-tensile steel.

If, on the other hand, the steel is required only for crack control it will normally be cheaper to use mild steel, which also has the advantage of being easier to cut and bend.

Where dense concrete is used, as described in § 9.2, the steel reinforcements will be adequately protected against rusting if they have 40 mm of concrete cover separating them from the external face of the concrete work.

If the reinforcements are allowed to come closer to the face of the concrete than this, there is a likelihood of moisture seeping through the concrete — particularly as the very presence of the reinforcement makes it more difficult to compact the concrete properly in this position. In rusting, the reinforcements oxidize to produce a far greater volume of material, and this pushes the thin cover of concrete off the main body of the foundation, so that further rusting can take place freely and at a very much greater rate. This in turn leads to yet greater increase in volume of the reinforcements, and may even cause actual splitting of the foundation. Certainly the area of full-strength steel will be diminished, as also will be the bond between the steel and the concrete. Thus it is important for permanent work to ensure that a minimum cover of 40 mm is provided to all reinforcements.

If, on the other hand, an excess of cover is provided, then the reinforcements will act less effectively in resisting bending moments than has been assumed in the calculations. This will lead to higher stresses in the steel, with consequent increased strains or stretching. And since the steel is now some considerable distance in from the face of the concrete, a given amount of stretch of the steel will cause a greater stretch or cracking of the concrete at the face of the foundation. Thus it is important to see also that the reinforcements do not have an excess of cover over and above the 40 mm.

In practice this means that reinforcements should be placed with extreme care so as to achieve a minimum of 40 mm cover to all steel on the one hand and a maximum value of 50 mm on the other to avoid too great a reduction in the effectiveness of the reinforcement. This can be achieved by using spacer blocks of concrete having the same quality as the foundation concrete itself or by supporting the steel on one of the proprietory forms of plastic spacer. Different contractors have different ways of doing this but it is important that proper attention is paid to the matter.

Index

Active pressure, 122, 127
adhesion of soil
    under retaining walls, 131
    to piles, 115
allowable bearing pressure, 5, 18, 19, 32, 56
angle of internal friction, 37
angle of repose, 10
attack by sulphates in ground, 146
augers, 23 24, 59

Balers, 23, 24
basalt, 11
base friction under retaining walls, 131
bearing capacity of
    piles, 114
    rocks, 14
    soils, 17, 18, 19
bearing capacity coefficient, 43, 45
bearing capacity
    safe, 14, 17, 18, 19, 43, 48
    ultimate, 31, 32, 43, 48
bearing pressure
    allowable, 5, 18, 19, 56
    on clay, 4
    safe, 56
bedding planes, 12
Bell's formula for earth pressure, 127
bending moments in
    independent bases, 81, 86, 89
    pile caps, 120
    rafts, 96
    retaining walls, 137, 142
    strip foundations, 78, 92
blinding, 75
bored piles, 104 *et seq*.
    design, 114
boreholes, 1, 19, 22, 24
boulders, 16
bulb of stress in soil, 52
buoyant foundations 7, 75

Cartwheel failure
    of retaining walls, 131

of spread foundation, 46
cast-*in-situ* piles, 104 *et seq*.
chalk, 11, 14
characteristic
    cube strength, 77
    load, 76
    strength, 76
classification of soils, 72
classification tests, 72
clay, 16, 18
    over-consolidated, 40
    normally-consolidated, 40
clay cutters, 23, 24
Code of Practice for
    foundations, 18
    structural use of reinforced
        concrete, 76
cohesion, 15, 35 *et seq*.
cohesionless soils, 16, 18
cohesive soils, 16, 42 *et seq*.
    laboratory tests, 61
cohesive strength, 37, 62
column bases, 81, 86, 89
column strip design, 92
compressibility
    coefficient of, 54
concentrically loaded column base, 81
concrete
    compaction, 144
    cover, 149
    mix, 145
    protection from frost, 148
    reinforcements, 148
    setting and hardening, 147
    slump test, 146
    workability, 146
consistency limits of soil, 72
consolidation settlement, 53
corrosion of reinforcements, 148
Coulomb's equation, 37
cover to reinforcements, 149

Depth of boreholes, 25
depth of foundation, 75
Design chart, 100